IN MY HOME THERE IS NO MORE SORROW

TEN DAYS IN RWANDA

RICK BASS

McSWEENEY'S BOOKS
SAN FRANCISCO

www.mcsweeneys.net

McSweeney's and colophon are registered trademarks of McSweeney's, a privately
held company with wildly fluctuating resources.

ISBN-13: 978-1-936365-99-9

Printed in Michigan at Thomson-Shore Printers.

IN MY HOME
THERE IS NO MORE
SORROW

TEN DAYS IN RWANDA

IN APRIL, THE LIGHT is beautiful in Rwanda—soft and warm upon the incredible new green that bursts from the fields and mountains, a living green that surrounds us as we near the end of the rainy season. The roads are filled with people walking. A very few ride bikes, and fewer still ride little motorcycles, but there are no cars other than our own. We have the road to ourselves, except for that endless stream of people coming and going on both sides, all of them carrying something—no work is ever wasted.

Every word I spend here without getting to the bones feels like I am shirking or betraying the obligation of witness. And yet, seventeen years after the fact, the thousand hills are greener than ever.

Still, if I do not begin with the bones—if they are not at least here on the first page—it feels wrong. I do not want this to be a travelogue, an irresponsible saunter through great beauty. Or rather, I do not want it to feel like any one of our other days, no matter where else we might be.

In 1994, during the genocide, hundreds of thousands of killers set themselves against hundreds of thousands of their fellow men, women, and children. Every village seems to have a memorial, the bones kept on racks and in rows, the time-cleansed skulls arranged neatly, an audience waiting for those who did not come—the long bones stacked to the rafters like so much firewood, casting latticed shadows. Because April is the anniversary of when the genocide began—of when the Hutu majority (85 percent of the population), fueled by hate radio, set itself against the Tutsi minority (which made up most of the remaining 15 percent)—purple and white pendants, symbolizing sorrow and mourning, surround each memorial. It is a month of pilgrimage.

At Ntarama, though, it's only us: my wife Elizabeth, our sixteen-year-old daughter, Lowry, the author and activist Terry Tempest Williams, who has invited us here, and me.

The memorial is a dirt-floor church, no longer used, but kept as it was to show what happened. In the warm sun, with the green fields of corn surrounding the place, you can still smell the faint odor of decay. The skulls and bones are the first thing you see; the wounds—the machete marks in the skulls—are the second.

It's disrespectful to look away, but of course you realize it's too late. The skulls are browned, not laboratory-bleached snow-white. *Where did all the rest go*, I wonder—*the hair, the eyes, the intestines, the skin, the fingernails?* The skulls are only part of the story; but they are more than we have preserved of our own wars and genocides.

There are more bodies buried out in the mass graves surrounding the church. Five thousand, six thousand, maybe?

But here in this tiny room—they must have been packed shoulder to shoulder—there are surely hundreds.

We're looking at them, but they're not looking back at us. Slowly, our gaze shifts to the left: to the dusty church pews, the dark-stained walls—stains everywhere—to the altar. There have been other genocides in Rwanda—1959, 1973, 1992. Students and teachers of history can come close, I suspect, to explaining the *how* and the *why*: the Belgian government, perhaps still run in some way by King Leopold's ghost, claimed "ownership" of Rwanda from the Germans after WWI, and chose to favor the Tutsi ruling class. The Belgians described the Tutsis as appearing more European; they made measurements to this effect. The repressed Hutu majority simmered, raged. Who fired the first shot can never be known. The killings, when they came, moved like a fever, a pulse, across the steep green mountains and through the verdant hills, the tension having reached some untenable peak; violence spilling out and over and down through the valleys, sowing hate and—the word I hear most commonly—evil.

What is understood about the 1994 genocide is that a single calculated event unleashed it: that the Hutu killers were at the ready, and waiting. (The Hutus had taken control of the country in 1962, in the same election that gave Rwanda its independence via referendum.) On April 6, 1994, the Rwandan president, an eventually peace-seeking Hutu moderate named Major General Juvenal Habyarimana, was assassinated by unknown actors; two surface-to-air missiles brought down his plane as it approached the Kigali airport. Most feel that Hutu extremists—adherents to the "Hutu Power" ideology, eager for an ethnically "pure" Rwanda—were behind the assassination, and had plotted to use it as a catalyst for the genocide. Others theorize that the killing was the work of Tutsi exiles in Uganda, refugees from previous genocides organized under the banner of the Rwandan Patriotic Front (RPF), who used the event to justify the RPF's re-entry into northern Rwanda. This latter theory does not seem to explain why Hutus began killing Tutsis all across the country within hours of the president's plane being shot down.

The Hutus had been preparing for the genocide, that much is known; Canadian lieutenant-general Roméo Dallaire, who led the UN's peacekeeping force in Rwanda between 1993 and 1994, had been warning the United Nations for months that the situation was about to blow. The night Major General Habyarimana was killed (along with the president of Burundi and ten others on the flight), hate-radio stations around Rwanda sent out the call, encouraging their Hutu listenership to exterminate all Tutsis, calling them *inyenzi*— cockroaches. The killing did not stop until more than a hundred days later, when the RPF (led by General Paul Kagame, who is now president of Rwanda himself) and Hutu Power groups negotiated a cease-fire. By then vultures were circling the country and bodies clotted nearly every creek and river. Bodies lay in every lake and along every road and path; they were stuffed into every latrine, dismembered. We traveled those same roads to get here, passing those endless streams of walkers, as if they were those same bodies come back to life.

They have not come back to life, of course. Their skulls are still here. They are not coming back.

The reason so many were killed in churches was that in the previous genocides, such structures had been a safe haven;

the *genocidaires*—the perpetrators—would not kill refugees if they were in a church. This time it was different. It's believed that the Hutu attackers, who included local militias known as *interahamwe*, allowed the refugees to flow into the churches until there was no more room, with both sides well aware of the expectation of sanctuary; then the *interahamwe* attacked.

The other common hiding place was the mosquito-ridden marshes, where the reeds and grasses were chest-high; marginal lands where the government had already begun to relocate the Tutsis, hoping to exterminate them silently, cleanly, through malaria and yellow fever. The killers were not willing to wait.

In the church at Ntarama, with no more listeners and no more sermons coming in this still and shaded place, not ever, we walk slowly away from all the waiting skulls. The militiamen tossed hand grenades through gaps in the adobe walls. Most of the windows are gone entirely now, though some are simply broken. The clothes of the departed are here, blood-sodden, laundered by death into a dense brown—all that vibrant color gone. You can't even call it red anymore; the blood on the walls is still red, but the clothes are just brown.

The shoes of the dead have been gathered up, too. The leather is cracked and worn, many miles having been walked to bring each person here, to this one place and point in time. Other artifacts are gathered on the church's shelves: clay pots in which they carried drinking water, for example, which are skull-shaped, and appear as fragile. A crude string, like a clothesline, is stretched in one corner; clipped to it like clothespins are half a dozen Bic ballpoint pens, the ink in them long since dried out. They look as if they'd been much-used, and it is this strange detail as much as any other, the datedness of these pens—the cheapest brand of Bic, the kind with the little blue plastic slip-on caps—that brings up the deep sorrow. The skulls, of course, but the pens, too.

These people were so poor. Rich in family and spirit but the poorest of the poor. The United States was running in the black that year, the great gearworks of our economy turning a billion-dollar profit, maybe a trillion, even, and we couldn't send three thousand peacekeepers, three thousand whatever, just to show the killers that this wouldn't be tolerated. We could have established a safe harbor somewhere; we could have done something. But six months earlier eighteen of our soldiers had died in Somalia.

I stare at those pens almost as long as I did at the skulls. I remember those pens being in vogue in the '70s; they're still bought and sold in bulk. Clearly, a missionary had brought a pack of them over at some point and passed them out. Was there time for any of their owners to write last-minute notes? Were there scraps of paper? What might they possibly have said?

The weapons that did the killing are on the floor, right by the broken shardglass window. They are small things, mostly, unexceptional: a curry-comb kind of apparatus, such as you might use to brush out a horse's tail. A file, a tiny knife—more of a letter-opener. A scythe. A small cannonball-like object, so small that a man could easily hold it one hand, smaller than a softball.

What was I doing, in April of that year? Turkey-hunting? Going to the gym? Mulling over a wine selection in the grocery store, or writing a little poem? In the meantime, people were walking barefooted for a thousand miles or more,

hiding beneath mountains of dead bodies, traveling at night—
the country set afire—to try to get to Burundi, to the south, or
Uganda or the Congo to the north; they were hiding in Lake
Kivu beneath vast mats of bloated bodies, breathing through
a reed, while in the mountains beyond, volcanoes erupted day
and night. What was I doing? It's easy to blame then-President
Bill Clinton—Madeleine Albright, his secretary of state at the
time, says that she lobbied for intervention as hard as she knew
how, and he could have singlehandedly stopped it. But so too,
I think, could we. Maybe. Certainly, we could have tried.

We walk up to another stucco building, behind the
church—a classroom. The floor is cluttered with broken
chairs. One corner of the small room is painted entirely red
with blood. This is where the children and babies were kept,
and when it was time to kill them it seems that the preferred
method was to swing them against the wall. Perhaps at the end
they huddled in that one farthest corner like minnows driven
to the last hiding place, into the shallows. What had anyone
done to deserve such horror? Was it just the unpardonable
sin of being favored, decades before, by the Europeans? Was
that what destined them for the ax, the machete, the grenade,
the bullet?

Throughout this narrative, there will be some mention of
the unmentionable, the unimaginable. To witness the evidence
of these things and then obscure or bury it from sight would
be to serve exactly the wishes of the killers. I will try not to
linger on images such as the wall where the babies were swung
by their heels and smashed. Wouldn't it be a little gratuitous
of me, to linger on such specificity seventeen years later? Too
offputting, pious-seeming, too little too late? That is not good

writing. And yet good writing is usually characterized by a crackling specificity. You hear the screams, you hear and smell the burning wood of the church, the sounds of the weapons striking their intended targets. In April, you smell the fear and the sap of the tree trunks that served as cutting boards, the trees lining the roads to these churches, their numerous machete-marks still not scarred over in the least. To omit all this is to patronize the reader.

I suppose I am looking for a small space, a localized triangulation somewhere between guilt, patronization, and the responsibility of witness. I do not know if I have found it.

A tour guide, a survivor, takes us slowly from building to building. A pair of pied crows—like our ravens, but with a corset or broad collar of white, like a priest's—roost in the rafters of the church, shoulder to shoulder, and stare down at us. There is a wooden sign next to the exit that has on it the words IYO UMENYA NAWE UKIMENYA NTUBA WARANYISHE: "If you'd known me and known yourself, you would not have killed me."

Suffice it to say that when we leave the memorial, we are walking more slowly, more subdued. We stop and sign the guest register, which has etched in it the word *Ntidigasubire*, "Never again"—which all governments, and all people, have said again and again, in all situations, throughout history, and yet *again* keeps happening, again and again—and then we drop our pitiful offerings into the donation box.

Back in our car—our gleaming tank of a car, loaded to the gills with our baggage, enough for four people for ten days—

we sit parked in the shade, stunned and reflective, listening to the singing of the birds and the happy shouts and cries of children. We do not ask it of each other, but there is no way that any of us are able to avoid the question—What is it that determines who is born where, and when? I remember as a child growing up in surburban whitebread Houston, being told to finish my vegetables. There were children starving in Africa who would have loved to have what I had, my father said.

And driving out, down the rutted red clay road that is redder than any I have ever seen, once again we pass slowly by the stream of people coming and going, each of them smiling at us and waving shyly, so that the boarded-over bridge in our hearts opens further and farther. We wave back to each of them, *maraho*, hello, with the exceptionally uncomfortable sensation that we are being treated like royalty. We cannot be invisible, no matter how hard we might wish or try to be. If they're this happy to see us now, how would we have been received back then, when we were needed most? For the life of me, I just don't understand what they see in me, what they see in us—who they have us confused with—to be so open and generous, so friendly. All right, I'll say it: so happy.

Where did the evil go? Did it seep back into the earth? Is it an organic, mortal thing, like the body itself? A thing that is born, arises, then dies and disintegrates, dissolves back into the ground, so that it lies—for a while—safely below us, though able always to be summoned or resurrected? Unsettling as that thought is, it is surely preferable to the alternative: that we carry the evil inside of ourselves, a virus that might lie dormant but that will always return.

The parade of color is vivid, refreshing: starched white

linen shirts, silk cerulean pantaloons, blue sky, gold parasols spinning slowly in the heat, perched atop the walkers' shoulders, the red clay road. Butter-yellow orioles fly back and forth in front of us, yellow across red, some of them carrying long streamers of yellowed grasses to weave into nests: again, the suggestion of festivity, with the faintest scent of rot still upon us—faint upon our skin and in our clothes, faint somehow in the woven cloth fibers of my watchband, mingling with the scent of our own living. The fields beyond so bright and verdant. Lacking the physical riches of the Congo, Rwanda's singular green beauty may be all it has to offer to the larger world, but it is enough, more than enough—everywhere, we will see signs of impending development, wealth from elsewhere, investment, construction, reconstruction. It amazes me how quickly a story can sink back beneath the surface, how quickly history can vanish, or be refined—*a million lives*—to but a sentence or three.

Let us continue.

We're driving on to the next genocide memorial, at Nyamata. I keep thinking about those Bic pens. So many of the bodies were identified by the clothes they were wearing; there was nothing else. Those particular arrangements of bright color—the garments dyed in red—were the only way for the survivors to know what had happened to their friends and family, their beloveds.

All along the road, such happiness, focus, purpose. A man walking with a thirty-five-foot limbed tree, a flexible green pole, balanced on his head, the trunk of the tree as thick around as his thigh, and tapering to a whip a few dozen feet away. Two men carrying a giant speaker, women carrying church pews, clearly on their way back from Easter Sunday service. Water, water; far and away, the most common load is water.

Three little girls in matching orange dresses walk with their arms around each other, a triptych of childhood innocence, sweetness, serenity, camaraderie. Here the boys and men walk hand in hand. It would sound like pathetic whining to suggest that Rwanda is in some ways richer than any of its betrayers— I would never say that—but I will say that I am astounded by the fact that the people here are not simply lying prostrate in the dust, paralyzed with depression, grief, anger, confusion. I don't know what I had expected. I guess I hadn't expected any of this. And certainly not the beauty: the broad marshlands in the valleys, the irrigated emerald rice fields, the misty volcanic mountains rising and falling in blue and green waves, the flanks so steep.

I might as well air it all out, here in my whiteness, my opening-heart, lucky to be alive and so blessed with health and the ridiculous affluence of what in America we would call a lower-middle-class economic strata: the babies and children are cute as the dickens. *Beautiful.* All babies and children are, but none more so than Rwanda's. There is some inner light that simply does not shut off.

Isn't that a horrible thing to say? It reminds me of my early years in the Deep South, and the ghosts of racism, cliché, stereotypes, the prejudice that still rose from the soil like mist in the summer after a hard rain on a hot day. *Oh, look at the cute little pickaninny*, says the grandmother in "A Good Man Is Hard to Find."

But I have to say it: I don't recall ever seeing a more beautiful people.

What does that have to do with anything?

Is it the Belgians' mistake, rewarding beauty—sowing the first seeds of inequity, tipping a balance, challenging the inner fabric of envy that resides in all humans?

It is all inexplicable. It is all horrific. It is all extraordinarily beautiful, and in our charmed car, passing by, we look out the windows at all of it, and wave, and wave.

I need to correct myself. When I described the passersby, the roadwalkers by the thousands, as being incredibly open, that wasn't exactly right: not at first. Almost all the children wave, interested in and sometimes fascinated by the big black SUV and the pale arms hanging out of the open windows—but the adults pass by with masks of a perfectly inscrutable countenance: watching you but not judging, offering neither hope nor condemnation nor anything else other than the calm dignity of attentiveness.

To a man, and to a woman, however, at the first utterance of a *maraho* by us, an *amakuru*, or even a *hello* or *good morning*, the masks break open, great friendliness is revealed—comes shining out—and we pass on with their faces opening before each greeting like blossoms opening to the light. Forgive the cliché. We are not the light, but they treat us as if we are the light.

For our daughter's sixteenth birthday, Terry has had hairdressers braid Lowry's beautiful long honey-colored hair into intricate cornrows, which give her the look of a local despite her northwoods whiteness; for the rest of our trip, people will stare and smile and touch and praise her hair, and praise the gesture of it: understanding, I think, how we might feel uncomfortable, and—unless I am reading too much into this—not wanting us to waste time or energy *being* uncomfortable, or guilty, or anything else that is wasteful and hollow and unproductive. The kindness, again, is all around us.

What I am feeling is not, I don't think, *shame*. You surely don't want to hear about that, and anyway I think it is something far more complicated. I think it is a combination of confusion, sorrow, and the light-filled relief—not quite joy, but relief—of the forgiven. In one part of you there is a lifting of the spirit—a new lightness, an airiness—while also somewhere within you there is a heaviness, something hard and mysterious becoming a little more dense. It is the feeling of the knowledge you have unconsciously or subconsciously sought to keep absent now finding a direct path or avenue to that place of density, heading there with the alacrity of iron filings clustering to a magnet. There's nothing in this life that you can do to make that place—about the size and shape of a palm-sized cannonball—go away. And the *worst* thing you could do would be to lament or rue the gift—the presence—of this new addition to it. To complain, to lament: Oh, how hard to carry around this extra little weight.

You carry it quietly. You say thank you for it. You try to hold the newness of it in you as you might hold a semiprecious stone. You do not toss it aside, you do not think or say, Oh, I wish my pack was empty. You walk on, a little unfamiliar, a little uncomfortable, a little honored.

*   *   *

It's not just the mothers who carry their babies—tiny babies—on their backs, swaddled with but a single towel; young boys and girls also tote infants, walking up and down the road, streaming to and from the water—sometimes a river, sometimes a well—and never, as best as I can tell, resenting or begrudging a single moment, a single instant, of life.

Such is the endlessness of their procession that it is the absence of motion that stands out in striking anomaly: the opposite of how it is in my country. I am used to the eye being drawn by, and fixing upon, movement, but here, instead, any stillness summons. An old man standing in the dark doorway of a stucco house. A young man—and we will see this only once—sitting beneath the shade of a tree, set some distance off the road, sketching in a notebook.

A wooden sign directs us off the main paved two-lane road (there are so few developed roads in Rwanda—the bare minimum, providing essentially a north–south and east–west corridor) and down the dirt road leading to Nyamata. Churchgoers are still streaming out from the village, in bright colors and shimmering finery, as if being expelled by the breath of God himself. They are still radiant in their fellowship, in the beauty of the spring day and in each other's company. As are we, the witnesses, each carrying now our small dense iron ball.

We park in the shade of yet another much-hacked tree. Here, too, purple and white pendants flutter, and here, too, the memorial is empty. It is in a much more contemporary church, a Catholic church built of red brick, with a high wrought-iron fence around a suburban-style newly mown lawn of St. Augustine grass. That such horrors might lie within it seems as improbable as the lawn is serene. We are the only visitors.

The sun is brilliant, though not yet hot—pleasant and soft—and on an adjacent dirt road we can still see churchgoers surrounding the even newer church a couple hundred yards away. Across the street from the memorial there are a couple of adobe houses; young men are milling around in the shade, tinkering with an upturned bicycle and playing festive hip-hop, a party beat that, in the splendor of the day, seems entirely natural, entirely wonderful, though again the old American self-consciousness arises as we draw nearer to the memorial and find ourselves navigating yet again that narrow seam between unimaginable horror and everyday beauty.

We pass through the first gate, the one that leads into the churchyard and approach the church. An elegant young woman in black slacks and a brilliant white longsleeved shirt, Elizabeth, greets us. In our country, I have no doubt, she would be an actress or a model, but here she is a genocide survivor and guide. She welcomes us quietly, steadily, explains the ground rules—no photographs—and as if willingly plunging into a nightmare, we enter the church itself, passing through the inner gate that once protected the churchgoers, its steel bars bent and pried open.

Inside there are no stacks and bundles of bones but instead all the clothes of the slain. It's a big church, and the first thing we notice are the myriad holes in the tin roof high above, perforations that allow pinholes of daylight to come strafing down at us, piercing the dark. There's no need to ask what they are.

The church is big, the size of a high-school gymnasium, and dome-shaped, round, with its highest point in the center; the roof slopes downward toward the perimeter of the circle. Elizabeth tells us that there were thousands of people inside when the attack came. "You might find it hard to believe," she says, "that you could fit so many people in here." But they kept coming. The *interahamwe*—the local militia who, up until the president's plane was shot down, had been friends and neighbors to the people here—allowed the church, like the one at Ntarama, to fill to the brim. Elizabeth says that at the very end, right before the killing began, some of the local Hutus lay down their arms and came into the church so that they might protect the Tutsis—or simply be with them—but it stopped nothing. They too were killed.

First came the grenades, and then the bars to the inner gate were pulled wide. The killers—and that is the word Elizabeth uses, with cold, steady clarity—squeezed through that gate one and two at a time, until a few who were inside were able to open it completely. Then the war, and hell, came flooding into the church.

All that violence is gone now. We have the vast space to ourselves. Only the brown-stained, bloodstiffened clothes are still here, folded neatly, as if awaiting a wearer who will never return. We walk toward the altar, toward the unharmed statue of the Virgin Mary up on the wall. The once white altar skirt is still soaked in blood. Blood is all over the ceiling here, back where the roof pitches down toward its outer edges; Elizabeth explains that the machetes sent fountains spurting up that high, and that body parts were found stuck to the ceiling as well, hanging there in gruesome disassembly until some days later, when the blood dried enough that its adhesive qualities subsided and the parts fell back to earth.

There were survivors. It was too much work to kill every one of them. Some, dismembered, were protected from further attack by the sheer volume of the dead and dying who fell on top of them.

You might have heard these stories before. Maybe you do not need me to repeat them. And in this, you might not be alone: in a forward-moving country like ours, possessed of its own horrific past of prejudice and bigotry, malice and terror, who would want to keep going back down into that basement? The United States has managed to make a pretty good living in this fashion for the last two hundred years, moving quickly across the backs of buried slaves and a very nearly eradicated native minority. Perhaps Rwanda's day in the sun will arrive as well. Perhaps the smartest strategy, from an economic standpoint, is to keep stories buried.

What, indeed, is the future of Rwanda? A tourism-based model, one that looks out at the endless mountains and volcanoes—some extinct and slowly disintegrating, others being born anew daily—while tiptoeing across the bones and the blood and the unvoiced, vanishing stories of genocide? Or does the country's future lie in exploiting its geothermal riches—the subterranean bubblings and hissings of barely buried fire? Or perhaps great mineral deposits, as in Rwanda's immediate neighbor, the Congo, exist, and have simply not yet been discovered? The high degree of volcanism might suggest the development of precious gems and crystals—even, perhaps, of diamonds.

Or perhaps the future lies in the incredibly rich soil, the

product of those decomposing volcanic plugs and necks—and, it must be said, also the product, in places, of those million bodies, all those bones and all that blood, all that joy gone back down into the earth. The ground here grows amazing crops; perhaps a system of high-value agriculture, of crops that are not easily grown elsewhere in Africa, might be a part of Rwanda's future. President Kagame, on the other hand, has spoken of his government's investment in broadband networks; perhaps Rwanda's future is a technological one.

Without question, though, whatever it turns out to be, this country's future lies in the hands of its young people—not just the survivors of the genocide but those born afterward, second-generation children who will grow up without having witnessed the terrible war. Depending upon their ethnicity, they might or might not have a feel for the stories. They will likely visit the memorials in April, as some in the American South visit the graves of Confederate and Union dead, or as those elsewhere visit Little Bighorn or Wounded Knee—but by and large, their lives will likely be less defined by tragedy than were those of their predecessors: which is, I think, the way we would all agree life is supposed to be. But given the cycle of violence here—the sporadic return of genocides, one spaced apart from another by four years, then ten, then two, then four, then two, then, mercifully, seventeen years and counting—the young people might wonder, sometimes, if in their lifetimes they too might experience that which so many others before them had to survive, or not survive. Perhaps it's like living next to an active volcano, one which they have never seen blow, but on whose now hardened lava they walk and laugh and play: the foundation upon which they have built their lives.

Here at Nyamata, our guide Elizabeth walks us slowly, steadily, through the church in practiced and professional fashion. She pauses at the altar to show us the tiny cross on a necklace sent to the church by Pope John Paul II, who had lobbied the United States hard, to no avail, to intervene against the genocide. Her voice is quiet and smooth, her countenance inscrutable, beautiful in the soft light, and yet each of us feels the weight of her experiences, her job, the story told yet again. She explains to us about the *Gacaca* courts, held after the genocide, in which participants came before the community they had harmed and confessed their sins with contrition. If their listeners believed them to be sincere, they were forgiven and provided amnesty; if not, they were returned to prison. But there simply weren't enough jails in the land to hold all the killers.

It was not an easy thing, Elizabeth tells us. *Can you imagine?* she says, so softly—as if her breath is leaving her—or perhaps she says *As you can imagine.* In either case, our mute answer is *No.* We shake our heads. "It is very hard," Elizabeth says, in that same quiet voice, barely more audible than a breath. Some of her strength seems to be leaving her. Her eyes close for a moment; she appears to be willing to herself to go on. "It is good for Rwanda," she says, "but it is very hard."

She sways: this beautiful powerhouse of a young woman. I want to reach out a hand to steady her. But she rallies. Through force of will alone she finds her center, opens her eyes, witnesses us standing there pale and essentially clueless, waiting on her, and, focused again, she says, "Let us continue."

There is a tile basement in the back of the church, a baptismal-font kind of place, or so it seems. I can't tell if it was part of the original church or if it was constructed after the genocide. The tiles gleam white, all is white, and the noon sun pours down through a skylight to illuminate yet another collection of skulls, these housed in a giant glass case, like museum specimens. Elizabeth's voice is so quiet that I'm having a hard time hearing her; I have to step in close, and still the words seem to me to be coming from very far away.

Most of the skulls bear the telltale signatures of trauma—some blunt, others sharp. Elizabeth is saying something about these particular skulls—why, out of a million, these sixty or so were chosen for the glass case in the baptismal light—but I'm too overwhelmed to record it. I feel like a bad witness, but somehow I just have to let some of it go, have to let it wash over and through and past me. I stand there and stare at the case—one of the skulls has a name written on it in magic marker, PATRICE, or PATRICK, I can't quite tell—and I know I should ask about it, but I'm shutting down. It's all I can do to just look, here in this strange new world, this strange new light.

We peer down to an even lower level, an illuminated basement beneath the all-white sunlit basement we're currently inhabiting. Far below us—ten, twelve feet?—and inaccessible, lies a wooden coffin with a cross resting on it, and a necklace of dried flowers. With great reverence, Elizabeth begins telling us the story of who is in it, but again my hearing fails me. I can only hear fractions of sentences, portions of words. The story is truncated, vanishing in time. The woman was pregnant, that much I can hear. There was something about a stick.

Lots of pregnant women were tortured; I'm not sure why this one, and her unborn or newborn child, merit this special lower level of illumination, deep in the core of the church, and, forgive me, I don't think I'm ready to know. An American lightweight, is what I feel like, adept at accumulating and schlepping physical things but not so good at carrying a share of global awareness and responsibility that is in any way proportionate to either my affluence or my consumption. I'm toting all the emotion I can handle right now, which is not, I fear, all that much.

When Terry asks Elizabeth if she thinks it could happen again, Elizabeth does not immediately reply. I had hoped, I realize, for a quicker response, and one in the negative. What she finally says is *Not like before*. She doesn't sugarcoat it for us. There are still people who harbor the old animosities, she says carefully; I do the math for the first time and understand that Elizabeth must be a survivor. No one escaped. Some kept living, but no one escaped.

Terry asks Elizabeth if she thinks President Kagame is doing a good job. Elizabeth pauses, not out of ambivalence, but as if to stress how impossible the task is. He is doing the best that anyone can, is her message. *It can be very hard*, she says.

Up top, back at ground level, Elizabeth shows us still another section of the church, this one set off at some distance from the others. On the pews and benches, more of the now too-familiar blood-brown clothes have been neatly stacked, never to be cleansed. But these set-apart clothes are different, a little more rumpled, with an unpleasant odor to them, even all these years later.

"So many of the victims were thrown down into the latrines," Elizabeth says.

I have never fully understood people, not even myself, but I feel that I know far less now—not more—than before I came to Rwanda. Under certain conditions—repression, generations of hatred, extreme poverty—and with some catalyst, anything is possible. I'd always heard that, and had read it in books—but I had never fully believed it.

It's not even the hatchets and machetes that lead me to this sad truth. It is instead the madness of swinging babies against one certain wall in a church, a wall dedicated by the killers for that purpose. It is the fact of those killers going to the extremely difficult trouble of stuffing all the latrines in Rwanda full of the slaughtered and the nearly slaughtered.

How useful is testimony? *Never forget. Never again.* How many times has the world said that before?

This might be a good moment, if a belated one, to mention what the hell I'm doing over here, and why I've brought my wife and youngest daughter. I cobbled together several reasons for the trip: Terry, for one, asked if I might be able to help teach a writing workshop she's volunteered to conduct at the National University of Rwanda, in Butare. (Before the genocide, there were three NUR campuses around the country; now there is only the one.) Terry and her husband Brooke sponsored a young man from Rwanda, Louis Gakumba, as a student in America, and subsequently adopted him into their family; Louis graduated from the University of Utah last spring, and has helped coordinate the workshop, though he was unable to join us on this trip.

We have also reserved a guide, for later on in the journey, to go see the mountain gorillas, up in the rainforest of Virunga National Park. And Terry, who has taken a shine to Lowry, acted as a mentor to her and a friend, made a special effort to encourage our daughter to come as well. As a school project, Lowry has secured dozens of brand-new running shoes, some donated by Nike and others by a local store in Missoula, the Runner's Edge, to distribute to orphans in the Twa pygmy village, just outside of Gisenyi. My publisher, in turn, has donated a hundred copies of one of my books, *Why I Came West*, and Terry has brought a hundred copies of one of her own, *The Open Space of Democracy*, as well as a few dozen of her latest, a book written about Rwanda, *Finding Beauty in a Broken World*.

And yet: why are we here? I cannot quite say. It's not much of an answer to insist that when Terry asked if we would like to accompany her, we simply said yes, and then set about combining a couple of small writing assignments (and this rather large one) and a lot of frequent-flier-mile donations and no small amount of cash from friends who supported one or another of the mixed bag of elements that make up the thin underpinnings of this journey. Those reasons are not really reasons; they're more like paper representations of some deeper meaning.

But if I cannot say why we are really here, then perhaps that is as close to a truth as any: that we were asked by someone to come, and that this time we said yes.

We leave the church, and walk back outside into the sunlight. Elizabeth shows us the grave of a human-rights activist, a sister in the Catholic church who warned of the coming genocide and who was killed the month before it began: assassinated by Hutu extremists who were evidently worried she might be able to influence the international community into intervening. She wasn't the only one who could have, of course: experts on the ground, including some in the military, knew it was coming. And yet it seemed unstoppable. As if all the rest of the world was paralyzed by a curious trance, a dark spell cast. Or it may just be that some countries are easier for the world to ignore than others.

What to do about it? It might take a hundred years, or five hundred—it took nearly half a century for the killing fever, the genocide pustule, to swell; there's really no telling how long the recovery might take. The Rwandan way, the Gacaca courts, the memorials, is not how we have chosen to deal with civil wars and genocides and massacres in our own country, but, uncomfortable as it is to witness, I think they have made the right choice. Not to bury the past, but to keep it in plain sight, illuminated.

We walk around to a new pavilion behind the church. It's the kind of place where, in our country, after-service church socials might be held—potlucks, maybe even outdoor weddings—but on second glance, I realize that it's not a picnic area at all, but the top of a vast underground mausoleum. The concrete is newly poured.

Elizabeth tells us that there are fifty thousand bodies here. That after the genocide, survivors scoured the roads and villages and brought all of the bodies they could gather to the church, as if the church would know what to do with them. Which it did.

Lowry, my wife, and I descend a staircase that leads inside. Terry, having seen it before, chooses to stay above, visiting quietly with our guide. And again, descending into the cool dark of the basement, I have to wonder what kind of parent I am, bringing my daughter in the week of her sixteenth birthday down into such a place. In a perfect world, don't we all want to protect our children's innocence just a while longer? To allow them as many days of halcyon splendor as possible?

The smell is a little stronger here, a little ranker, in the closed-in confines. The mausoleum is cinderblock, and a split-level storm window lets in just the faintest slant of green light. The passageway between bookshelves—there are bookshelves down here, to hold the remains—is so tight that our elbows and shoulders are brushing against them. We are swimming through a sea of skulls, and we are as speechless as the skulls themselves.

Back up top, something seems to have changed in Elizabeth-our-guide. She seems more rested, more relieved, and I know that Terry has been asking the hard woman-to-woman questions that I would have shied away from. What was the genocide like for you, who did you lose, what do you really think of Kagame, do you really think it could all happen again? And earning, with her interest, a slow trust. Does anyone else who comes through here ask such questions? Or do they only absorb this woman's rote and somber testimony with the passivity of a packhorse, allowing themselves to be saddled with some unknown weight in preparation for the morning's long trek toward an unfamiliar destination?

It's not in her job description to ask us what we think, or to tell us her own story—but her visit with Terry while the rest of us were down in the bone room has stirred some trust in her. She tells us a little of her story now—that friends of her family, Hutu *interahamwe* members, turned on Elizabeth and her people in that fateful hour when the radios called out for it. Elizabeth has published an essay about her experience, which I'm able to read later on, and in it, the sense of a seven-year-old girl's betrayal and confusion rings strong. But we're haunted, too, when we read her account, by her assertion that she was one of the lucky ones, in that she didn't have to see her parents being killed; they were taken away first.

So many of the testimonies speak of how, if the Tutsis were formerly friends with or acquaintances of their murderers, they could sometimes buy a quicker death—paying the murderers to shoot them rather than torturing them.

We want to believe such atrocities could occur only in this one tiny landlocked country—that such terrorism is unique to this one garden-spot on earth, ringed by mountains, unbounded by any shining sea or navigable river. We cannot own this. It is either the singular landscape's fault—the rainforests and the volcanoes, and some shimmering, hissing secret in the soil—or it is an experiment, a mistake off the tree of life, one that we are fortunately not connected to, and never were, and never, under any circumstances, will be.

Those are the only two possibilities. Landscape as villain, or Rwandans are different. The third possibility—that the potential for evils is within all mankind, just as the potential for great good is in all mankind—seems too hard to accept.

Elizabeth pauses at the edge of the shade offered by the pavilion above the mausoleum, talking to us now as a friend, as the young woman she is. In her black slacks and sparkling white dress shirt, she looks like a movie star. It seems as if all the bones just below us—fully 5 percent of the one million slaughtered in '94—are her audience, are listening attentively to her quiet voice, which is so thoughtful and considered that it sounds almost sleepy. Elizabeth was a teacher, right out of college—she studied science and education, then taught biology to elementary-school students before taking this job— and when she mentions her essay again, and tells us that she would like to become a writer, we ask her to please consider coming to our workshop in Butare the next day.

It's short notice, but she doesn't hesitate. She really wants to write. Her eyes do not so much widen as momentarily dilate—life can be curious and quick, opportunity can present itself like the shadow of a bird passing before the sun, present then gone—and she says that if she can find someone to substitute for her at work for the next couple of days, she'll join us there. She hasn't heard of the writing club we'll be speaking to, but why should she have? There is no publishing world in Rwanda, no literary association, no anything—only scattered writers, penning their thoughts and images in isolation, as writers have always done. Our guide gives Terry her cell-phone number, and we give her the contact information for the president of the writing club, a young man named Amini. For the first time it feels like we're useful, like we have something to give besides our mute and belated—useless, actually— skull-witnessing. In our wan little personal lives, it's the first time we've felt good and clean about being here.

Once again we wander stunned back to the luxury SUV we've borrowed for our sojourn. I notice that the vibrant dance music that was blaring across the street when we first arrived has been turned down, the playlist switched to something softer, classical-sounding—something Easter Sunday–ish—and this delicacy, this graceful gesture of acknowledgment, touches me.

Once again, we sit quietly in the car, staring out at the red clay road, the gardens crowding either side of the lane, the violent markings on the big tree in whose shade we're parked. It's not so much a lethargy that has descended upon us, as instead a need to rest and process—to accept—what we've seen and heard.

We sit for a long while, visiting quietly, and I do not mean to make it sound like we have it so hard, having to shoulder such knowledge. I am not complaining. I am only marveling. I am stupefied.

We're not ready to go back to the bustle of Kigali. Instead, we turn south and travel farther on, down toward Burundi: deeper into the country. The endless tides of humanity are still walking, all of them carrying improbable loads on their heads and in their hands; those who are riding their old single-speed bicycles labor beneath even more, loads so ponderous—eight jerry-cans of water; an entire kitchen-length of cabinets; a load of bricks—that their bike tires are squished flat. They are all conversing and smiling and laughing, proceeding into the day with purpose and meaning, as if utterly unattached to— severed from—the past. We, the Americans, continue to drift.

I can't help but look at the landscape in terms of escape. Where would I have gone, seventeen years earlier? What would I have done? My instinct would be to get up into the mountains, the jungle—to climb a tree and hide, for a hundred days, or however long was necessary, coming down only for water at night, or to hole up in a cave, or to dig a pit and cover it with branches—but getting there would not have been easy, all the fields recently cleared, even the narrow valleys a few miles wide, with so many other people compressed into those open spaces. Perhaps the tall marsh grass would have been better. Terry tells us the story of one young Tutsi woman who made it up into the mountains—an athlete in the Olympics. As she was running she caught a glimpse of a silverback gorilla, startled by her, running in the other direction. Terry tells us, too, that after the cease-fire was signed it was the RPF that went out into the marshes to gather up those who were still in hiding: the soldiers wading through the water and calling out that it was safe now, that the war was over. Surely some of the refugees would not have believed it—would have thought it was a ploy. Others who did come out were too weak to stand, were injured or debilitated, and needed to be carried back to dry land.

For a pacifist such as myself, it's important to remember that the cease-fire was accomplished by war; that the Rwandan Patriotic Front's counterattacks on the Hutu military are what brought the Hutus to the table, a hundred days after the genocide began. The Hutu extremists' goal was to wipe out all the Tutsis, or, failing that, the entire fledgling generation of them: and they very nearly did it. A million fatalities in a hundred days. The Tutsis had to save themselves, with force. No one came to help them.

We're driving slowly, and down the center of the road, to give safe space to the throngs on either side. Even out here, farther into the country now, there are throngs. No one is resting. Everyone is moving. We're driving so slowly that the butterflies swirling in front of us have time to veer out of the way; they flutter up toward the windshield, pulled into the slipstream of our approach, but then with paper wings are able to right themselves and fly away, unscathed.

We're thirsty and a little jittery. The little yellow tin signs advertising Primus beer that are tacked to various open-doored stucco buildings in the tiny villages we pass through look appealing, and Lowry agrees she would drink a Coke, but we can't quite figure out which if any buildings are taverns and which are just regular homes with Primus signs on them. We're a little hesitant to just pull up to any old building and ask for a beer. So instead we drift on, unfamiliar and off-balance, until finally our thirst exceeds our shyness and we turn down a broad alley where dozens of children are playing. We pull up in front of a brightly painted blue-adobe building; numerous men—some young, some old—are sitting out front, some in the shade and others in the sun. If this isn't a bar, I don't know what a bar is.

Our car gleams like a polished black meteorite. We step out, feeling crippled by our glaring affluence, our conspicuous whiteness—we crave anonymity, but on this trip we will not find it—and walk inside as if we know what we're doing.

It's dark in there, and men as well as several women are packed in densely, seated in plastic chairs and watching a soap opera on the television that's been mounted in one corner of the bar. We'd be happy to sit inside, but instead we are escorted through the room to a narrow patio out back. It's an open-aired but closeted kind of place, each table in a sort of private cubicle—and once we are thus secluded (though there are no other diners in any of the other closet-cubicles), our drinks are brought to us. We sit in this isolation and enjoy each other's company, watching the beautiful towering cumulus clouds build billowy white beyond the edge of the tin roof above, higher and higher into the blue sky. We imagine the meals that have been taken in these cubicles—there are two rows of them, one on either side of a concrete aisle—and we imagine that on a Friday night it can get pretty fierce.

As is so often the case with Americans abroad, the crutch of our privilege—in this case, relying upon the world to speak our language—inhibits relationships, keeps them at a safe if not thoroughly satisfying arm's-length distance. For example, we've ordered Primus, but we mistakenly asked for the quart-size tankards, not the svelte little bottles, so that we are awash in beer. As the driver, I can only watch forlornly as Terry and Elizabeth—my wife Elizabeth, not our guide—imbibe. Lowry doesn't escape this confusion, either; as often will occur on the trip, she is mistaken for an adult, and a beer is set before her, in these few days following her sixteenth birthday.

A cheerful young man with a cell phone joins us. We've learned some basic phrases, how to introduce ourselves and ask the name of a stranger—and he tells us that the owner of the bar has called him to come interpret for us: that he's the only fluent speaker of English the bar owner knows. We're told that only last year did the first *muzungus*—which is what white people are sometimes called, but which, more specifically, refers to rich people—come to this off-the-beaten-path establishment, and that we are only the second such group ever: that it's been a full year since the first thirsty *muzungus* dared stop, and that no others have followed them until now.

Our friend's name is Guthvalence—or that's how it sounds to me, with my damaged hearing. He asks us if we would like some meat.

We're not particularly hungry, but we tell him we would. He hurries back to the kitchen to relay our order, and then returns.

I'll try not to caterwaul too much about the woes of not being invisible. It's quite possible that anyone we encounter here would be thrilled to trade places: to assume that burden of affluence and power, if not strength. Some loud '70s tune is playing in the bar now, and when we gesture to Guthvalence that we like it—we're laughing at how loud it is—he thinks we're complaining that it's *too* loud, and dashes into the bar to tell the owner. Seconds later, the volume is dialed down to a discreet and very un-barlike Muzak croon. When Guthvalence comes back, we try to convey that we were just laughing, was all, that in no way do we want to impose our desires upon the folks in the bar, but we're unable to make ourselves understood. The previously festive, even raucous music remains subdued, in deference to the gigantic micromanaging of the high-maintenance Americans.

A little while later, Elizabeth-my-wife walks out into the courtyard to take some pictures—the blue sky with those towering snow-white clouds, the yellow stucco of the partitioned outdoor dining cubicles with their elegant, spartan tables. A simple room with four chairs, so that we're able to focus on the triumvirate of food, drink, and conversation with that blue sky above, the pied crows occasionally passing back and forth. While she's gone, the chef appears, showing us, with great pride, the newly severed head of the kid goat that has just been terminated on our behalf.

Even to the Montanans among us, it's a little outside the norm. The machete, at least, appears to have struck the goat so forcefully that there was no discomfort, no realization that the blue sky or the sunlit springtime day would ever end—and a short while later we are sharing shish kebab, which there can be no denying is delicious and tender.

What is the essence of joy, what is the essence of melancholy? Do not the two share the same root, twisting and writhing, reforming and metamorphosing in braids and strands like rising smoke, one defined perhaps by the absence or even the faint leavening of the other, caterpillar-and-butterfly? One moment ago—one precise *moment* ago—I had been feeling a pure and unadulterated peace, a deep contentedness and relaxation that was safely just this side of out-and-out joy—and then suddenly, with the speed of a blade falling, there was a shadow and a shift; I blinked, and all things had an echo of sadness, even horror. The sword that had cut off the goat's head could well have maimed and killed dozens or hundreds of humans, scant years earlier—indeed, for all I know, the arm that did the swinging could have practiced that same motion on its fellow men. The chipped wall of our cubicle— the exfoliating stucco—could be blamed on bullets, not the slow erosion of time, and the specks and splatters of paint on the floor could just as well be blood. Even the deafening drumming of the hail above us—and yes, as we are eating, a violent hail sweeps suddenly across us, banging down on the tin roof so loudly that we cannot make ourselves understood to one another even by shouting—could as easily be machine-gun fire, opening the ceiling to the stars at Nyamata. Was I a fool, for briefly inhabiting peace? How can seventeen quick, thin years actually separate the world's worst horror from such a lazy, leisurely Sunday afternoon in the same place, among the same people?

Let me dig a little further: how can a people who have endured—survived—a hundred days of such atrocity, or a hundred years, find peace, or—the further and perhaps less stable territory—joy? How can they, who have so little, and from whom almost everything has been taken, walk down the road smiling, or sally into our cubicle to visit with such bonhomie? How can they be so delighted to make our acquaintance, to practice their English with us, to show us the head of a goat?

I can understand the children being that way. I understand that there is an effervescence, an elixir, in the blood of all children, and indeed almost all young things. But this resilience appears to transcend that. Is my own country so depressed that to simply be away from that milieu is so striking?

I am not articulating it clearly. After just twenty-four hours in Rwanda—but having encountered, already, what must be tens of thousands of people—it occurs to me that I'm passing through the midst of a phenomenon.

It feels not so much like another country as another universe, another time, and, I have to say it, like we are in the presence of spirits superior to our own: less numb, less jaded, less beset by self-focus and the low chronic agony of unmet desires, many of which do not even originate within us but have been grafted on from the outside. Under any circumstances—genocide be damned—such freshness of spirit, whether in the green spring or any other season, would be notable, an exception valuable for its rarity. But given what has blossomed here previously—the pustulous expulsion, the heated, fevered breath and essence of hatred—well, it's all the more phenomenal.

I know it's sinful to be thinking this way—to be envious of anyone in Rwanda, while lamenting the fogginess, the numbness and belly-focus that has swept across my gilded homeland—and that's not what I mean to be saying. Let me just stop it at this: there is a spirit moving through Rwanda that is profound and surprising. It is a spirit of what most people would probably call *love*.

I'm not saying that's the whole of it. What I suspect is that there is probably not a word for it—the feeling, the spirit, the phenomenon—and that none of us on the outside of it, thank God, will ever quite know what it is; not seventeen years later, and not ever. I wouldn't, on reflection, trade my numbness for what they have. Even an arm's-length distance might be a little too close. It's kind of terrifying to witness such capacity for strength, for spiritual growth; who among us would not prefer, really, to remain flabby, vague, untested?

The storm passes. We finish our sacrificial goat. We leave our Primus bottles half full, say our good-byes and thank-yous, and walk back through the dark crowded bar and into the sunlight, where children are playing, barefooted, laughing and shrieking, in the storm's new puddles. If joy and terror, or love and hatred, can come from the same red soil, or from within the same human soul—the same genetic architecture of our species— what then might correlate or twin or twine with the twisting feeling of guilt that discomforts us? How might we turn or escape it? I imagine it is not easily bought, not easily altered. Easily forgotten or buried, yes, but not so easily transformed: and again, what that thing's opposite might be, I cannot yet say.

*   *   *

We drive slowly back to Kigali, marveling at the humanity—the utterly unique disparity, in our view, between so many people and so few vehicles of any kind. It's all muscle power. A few older women are hoeing out in the bright red-ribboned fields, the furrows new-turned and recently planted, so that there are only sprouts and seedlings arising—and the cumulus clouds build again, the sky-belly rends open and dumps democratically upon us all, drenching the newly furrowed soil and the road and the pedestrians, some of whom take refuge beneath the nearest tree while others march resolutely on. The scattered motorcycles proceed as well, if more slowly, their riders' heads tilted, tucked. Great globes of raindrops are falling so hard and close together and onto such a quickly flooding surface that they bounce like ping-pong balls. Everything is different here, even the rain.

We stop on a low ridge overlooking the broad valley of the Nyabarongo River, and the marshes where so many of the Tutsis hid. There is a similar marsh near our home in Montana, and when our daughters were very young we would play a game with them called "Tiger in the Grass": they would run into the marsh's center—this would be in late summer, when the marshgrass was dry and high and rustly, the sedges and grasses taller than the girls—and hurl themselves into the wilderness of it, burrowing into warrens and labyrinths and self-made tunnels, having been given a headstart count of ten before we went searching for them, calling out, sometimes drawing very close to them without knowing it and other times veering away from their hiding spot—filling them proportionately and accordingly with delicious waves of fear and exultation. And when they had gauged that we, the searchers, had drifted far enough past that they could jump up and run for the safety of home base (of home itself, in this case), they would: shrieking and laughing, stumbling and falling, floundering and flouncing in the cushioned jungle of the tall dry grass, the blades of which would sometimes slice our arms with tiny stinging paper cuts that at the time were unnoticeable, infused as we all were with the adrenaline of the chase.

While we're stopped, looking down at the Rwandan marsh—nobody appears to be living in it now—from the comfort of our car, a group of young boys approaches the rain-gleaming black spaceship we've appeared in. They perch on the running boards, and I roll down the window to visit. They're not asking for anything; they just want to show off their English. Since 2008, they tell me, English has taken the place of French as the primary language in the schools here. How quaint, I think; how touching. Why not Chinese? Who makes these singular decisions, these pivot-points that will end up affecting the lives and welfare of so many? *They believe in us*, I think. *They still believe in us*. These boys, between the ages of six and twelve, would be the children of the genocide survivors, second-generation survivors—and my heart wobbles and skitters a little, I can't shake easily the tiny, edgy stirring—the worry—that they are making a big mistake: that we are not worthy.

I suppose we still have some say in the matter. You can't look at it in terms of making amends—no amount of deeds, or labor, or even the passage of time, can re-tilt that ledger— but if there's something you have to give, beyond your respect and sympathy and attention, better then to give it than not.

Internationally, of course, it's becoming a vexing problem; the old model of missionaries and other humanitarian organizations shipping goods—clothes, mostly—to African villages has been questioned recently, with rising concerns that these gestures run the risk of creating permanent cycles of random subsidy that—so goes the theory—become only a kind of obstacle to economic development. Better, goes the theory, to invest in local businesses that manufacture shoes, rather than offering shoes for free and thus preventing such a business from existing at all. The world, according to this new line of thinking, has been locking Africa in the trap of continued colonization: a well-meaning but ultimately debilitating practice that has built an intergenerational culture of dependency upon philanthropy, meager though it is.

Everywhere you see evidence of it. Some of it is dramatic— the community clean-water wells, to and from which all travelers trek daily—and the clothes, particularly the T-shirts, so clearly Goodwill-provided. *Becky's and Don's Fiftieth Wedding Anniversary, Pocatello, Idaho, 1978. Klamath Falls Bowling League Championships, July 4, 1990*. Etc., etc.

I don't know enough about the issue to feel I'm able to offer a correct answer; I would imagine the answer is *both*, the answer is *everything*. Some historians believe the twenty-first century will be the Century of Africa, due to youth demographics and resources. I have my doubts; foreign investment, largely in the form of China (funded by America's debt, due to our insatiable appetite for plastic crap), is purchasing huge deposits here of rare minerals, oil, water, land. But I believe in story, and the first-story of Africa being formed from an initial wound— the great slab of Gondwanaland rifting apart, separating as if cleaved along the tectonic plates, the world's fire, in all its terrible beauty, roaring up from beneath and creating a new land, a new garden—may play itself out over and over again. Where once Africa was a garden, surely it will and must be again.

In the meantime, not knowing any better, and not knowing what else to do, we have brought with us those thirty new pairs of tennis shoes. It's a very American response, I think, to want to believe we can fix anything—that no wound or crevice is too vast, that we are still all-powerful. It is unfortunate that we are able to stand by while such wounds are created, but there exists always, in our minds, the opportunity and capacity for redemption.

This is ludicrous, of course—again, the equation does not balance—and yet our old hungry habit persists. It is human nature to want to blot up the spill, to right the tipped vase, to sweep up the broken shards. To cleanse, and obscure the evidence of one's great clumsiness.

What do we have to give to these people? Hopefully something more than thirty pairs of shoes.

There were other genocides. I recall dimly from my youth that this was so. I was too young to know of the one in 1959, but remember now hearing that it had occurred. As a child in whitebread Texas, when I heard that in a country called Rwanda, tribesmen called Tutsis and Hutus were fighting each other—slaughtering each other—I confess to envisioning the killing taking place not with machetes and machine guns but with spears and poison darts. It seemed unfathomably far away. I confess to not considering, in elementary school, that the combatants were loving people with close-knit families and deep spiritual traditions and beliefs. I assumed that Rwanda was an anomalous part of the world, a place beyond redemption, a place that fortunately had nothing to do with us.

There was another genocide in 1973. I would have been about Lowry's age. I remember that one being a paragraph in the newspaper, a single headline on the evening news. Watergate and the end of Vietnam were the limited focus of current events in my adolescent world. Civil wars in Africa, resource squabbles, tribal animosity—none of this had anything to do with us. It was unfortunate, it was sad, but it was the way the world was. Again, I assumed that because the country was embroiled in such violence, there was no hope for it to be otherwise; it was simply the way things were, back in the jungle. Some places, and some people, were simply more savage than others.

That was the last of my excuses. I don't know where I was during the genocide in 1990, or during the one in 1992, or even during the big one in 1994, right after Somalia. I'm not going to beat myself up about it anymore—no one person can save a million others; there is a momentum to history and a dark throbbing, an evil, in the hearts of men that no light can entirely dissipate, and which I certainly am incapable of dissipating singlehandedly—but I do have to say it: by 1994, I was old enough to know better. These were not wild animals fighting in the jungle; this was hell opening up through a vent, a great rift, in the large organism of humanity, and we all simply turned away. I can't quite get over that. The survivors appear to have gotten over it, somewhat, but for we newcomers to these fields of bones—these emerald fields so recently and continually fertilized with the blood and bones of human beings—well, we have some quiet time ahead of us. 1994 is ours; we own it. By turning away—by choosing to not look at it—it became tied to us forever.

We drive back to our cushy hotel in the capital, back into the flow of commerce. Giant cranes rise above the city's skyline, particularly along the desirable ridgeviews. The banana plants out in the fields, their large droopy leaves rain-slashed as if by blades, flap in the wind and glisten from the new rain. We pull up behind a giant transport truck in which numerous sheaves of dry tobacco appear to be hanging. The truck hits a bump and all of the previously motionless sheaves stir to motion, and are revealed, like a mosaic being slightly disassembled, to be a jumble of arms and legs, soldiers in camouflage, each with one arm holding on to the bar overhead. They are wearing dark berets and carry black machine guns slung over their shoulders, and their faces are as dark as charcoal. They all stir at once, regathering their balance, and in so doing they remind me of a hibernarium of monarch butterflies, the great cluster of them, all their wings flapping slowly to generate a pulse of collective heat before stilling again: a chrysalis of war, or—one hopes—of defense, able to prevent, this time, next time, any time, the return of what's come before.

If a million were killed, and less than 15 percent of the 8 million men and women living there beforehand were Tutsi, how many survived? You can't help but wonder how many were left, hiding in the forest, in the rivers and lakes, in the closets and beneath the beds, in the attics and in the rubble of churches and in the marshes, beneath the disassembled body parts of their neighbors, their families… A hundred thousand, two hundred thousand? A tiny number. They were almost wiped out. There was already a diaspora from the previous genocides. This was almost extinction.

One of the things I find most haunting, as I've said, is that everyone in Rwanda kind of knew it was coming. In her memoir, *Left to Tell*, Immaculée Ilibagiza writes of how it was known that assassination lists existed, and that hate radio had been preparing the Hutus for violence; her family even stayed up the night before the genocide began, discussing the rumors her brother had brought to them. He wanted to flee the country that night—to cross giant Lake Kivu, to the other shore and the sanctuary (at that time) of the Congo. They all talked about it, but in the end the hour was late, they were too tired, too sleepy. Maybe it will be all right, they told themselves. It had been a while since the last Tutsi massacre. The exile army was promising to come back over the border if necessary, and the president was holding peace talks. Hope was in the air. They went to bed that night, and in the morning it began.

The next day we go to the big genocide museum in Kigali. Unlike the churches out in the country, this one is crowded with visitors. Its elegant, contemporary architecture is designed with one focus in mind: the processing of grief. There are xeriscaped little alcoves, resting benches, reflecting areas, stained-glass murals, steps that gently ascend and descend.

Inside, it's a circular maze, with giant wraparound photos and posters and wall text and video loops, the history of Rwanda and the history of the genocides unscrolling in the dark, room by room, so that it feels endless—like you'll never emerge—and then when you finally do, climbing the long, gentle, winding steps up through the stained-glass light and back out into the brilliance of Rwanda's spring, you still carry with you some of the darkness. You have the knowledge of the life-size photographs of sweet and innocent children, the million-dead figure replaced by one image after another, story by story. Thierry Ishimwe, a bright-eyed little boy, nine months in the world. His favorite drink, his mother's milk. Behavior: cried a lot. Characteristics: a small and weak baby. Cause of death: macheted in his mother's arms.

Fillette Uwase. Age two. Favorite toy: doll. Favorite food: rice and chops. Best friend: her dad. Behavior: a good girl. Cause of death: smashed against a wall.

Brother and sister, Yves Mugatha and Yvonne Uwer, five and three. Yvonne Daddy's girl, Yves Mummy's boy. Hacked to death at Grandmother's house.

Again and again I study the faces of the living: the survivors. Almost always, people look as if all of it is behind them. They give no evidence of possessing the stunned confusion, the spiraling-down dispiritedness, that attaches itself to me as I witness the residue, the stories. They appear to have moved on, and away.

A friend will tell me later of a cognitive-therapy technique where survivors of traumatic events create physical timelines using a piece of rope, a pile of rocks, and a pile of flower blossoms. The rope is the arc of their life; wherever they place rocks along it indicates the hardships and traumas. The flowers represent the good events. It sounds hokey, but evidently the success rate is phenomenal. The survivor has been carrying the trauma around—there is no yesterday, it is still and always present—but once the brain sees those rocks laid down in the past, it begins to rewire. The trauma has literally been pushed back and away, and for the first time, the healing can proceed.

I don't know if this has been employed in Rwanda. I don't know how they have done it.

Who has been healed? Seventeen years later, have all those who could not survive the trauma (and how could anyone?) been washed away, vanishing through the cracks of time and history as secondary casualties, brought down by a kind of death-without-dying that eventually does become a truer death? I just don't see anyone who looks all that haunted or depressed; I don't even see the drunkenness you might expect, the hazy self-medication of escapism. Perhaps, after seventeen years, only the resilient remain—survivors who survived even the surviving. Perhaps.

It's not that I want or expect them to go around keening, nearly a fifth of a century later. I don't mean to sound reproachful, or envious. In some ways, though, the presence of such easy equanimity—the casual joy and kindness—is as puzzling to me as the unmentionable evil that washed through, hopefully in one last grand exhalation, a final immolation of that element. It strikes me again: I think what I'm seeing is happiness.

* * *

We leave the genocide museum in Kigali and pick our way through the traffic, possessing no road map, stopping to ask directions often. I'm surprised by how cosmopolitan it is, how it seethes with human energy: pedestrians and cars and trucks and bicycles everywhere, following the neat and ordered directions of roundabouts, on-ramps, and off-ramps; giant cranes swinging girders high above on the hills; tall buildings all aglitter. Commerce proceeds with its inimitable appetite. It is a relief to be putting it behind us.

We know our destination is south and west of Kigali, and there just aren't that many roads in Rwanda; once we're out of the capital city, we should eventually find ourselves on the way to Butare. There aren't any mileage markers or signposts, but everyone we ask keeps pointing us in the same direction.

People are still walking up and down the road; each day the ceaseless stream will not shut off until about nine or ten o'clock at night. We pass by various groups of woodcutters, each of which is felling or has felled the most amazing and immense eucalyptus trees I've ever seen. Some of the trees are being sawn into planks of rough-cut lumber right there on the spot, the limbs and leavings gathered for fuel or to make charcoal; charcoal here is cooked for days in apoxic smoldering huts, much to the detriment of the workers and villagers who breathe the smudge and in fact to the detriment of almost all life on earth. *Muzungus* such as ourselves drive our cars and ride around in jets, expelling and exhaling untold tons of carbon, and in Rwanda the charcoal-burners do their own small part as well, while life as we all know it changes year by year and day by day, or perhaps even hour by hour.

There is a structure to all stories, and to all journeys.

I think that the structure or shape of this story is that of a volcano, or of a mountain. Some of the mountains here are the remnants of old volcanoes that have gone cold; others still burn below, occasionally bubbling over and sometimes even erupting, rivers of glowing fire descending as if the hell prophesied by fundamentalist preachers has been made manifest. This journey—my little week's journey—seems to somehow be following the course below us, the course of the land, with a long slow flat approach to the mountains' base, at which point—soon—the heart and legs will pitch steeply upward, and the climb will begin. In leaving the rich valley floor and the seething masses behind, it might feel at first that we are moving away from our chosen territory. But I trust the shape of the land. When mystery is dominant, and no answers can be had, I think it makes sense sometimes to veer away from all the old places one has been tilling and exploring, and turn toward something even more unknowable.

I am speaking metaphorically now of steep mountains, some of which house deadly boiling magma and others of which do not—I am speaking metaphorically of the dense lush rainforests on the flanks of those old volcanoes. The devastation of those forests, the trees being cut down one by one as if in hand-to-hand combat, so that the wood can be scorched to charcoal, so that the charcoal-makers can survive another day (eighty percent of Rwandans live in rural villages), is leading to massive erosion; the rivers run as red now from loss of topsoil as they once did from blood. Mudslides, not Hutu–Tutsi violence, are now the leading cause of death in Rwanda. Millions of tons of some of the richest country in Africa are being swept away, spirited away in broad daylight, ferried downstream and across the borders. All along the road, the biggest trees are being felled.

There aren't many left—just a few isolated giants—but the scent of new-sawn eucalyptus, with oozing sap, is sweet and thick, invigorating, uplifting; it carries the exciting promise of possibility, of the industry of the mind. Once a tree is down, anything can be made from it; we are by nature an active, thinking, creative species, master manipulators. The scent of fresh sap stirs one of the deepest parts of us, as the scent of bread baking in the hearth does, or meat being grilled over an open fire. We drive past each fallen tree slowly—police with machine guns are supervising each operation, I'm not sure why—and it is only some days later that I remember the whispered code of the hate-radio stations, which unleashed the killers in the precise hour that President Habyarimana's plane was shot down: *Cut down the tall trees*.

I have been speaking metaphorically of a story that has traveled carefully and slowly through flat countryside, but which comes now to the first steep pitch of verdant, dripping mountains. Landscape as escape. We are following that path.

Once we reach Butare—a bustling town with rutted, bumpy roads, but vibrant, clotted with throngs of dazzling men and women, all dressed brightly—we check in at the Hotel Ibis, which has a delightful open-air streetside café and, with its lazy patio-ceiling fan, an exotic Casablanca feel to it. It occurs to me, as we settle in and I make one last attempt to understand where we have been, that depression may sometimes simply not be a biological option—that the wounds and trauma of having the gates of hell open up and pour out across the land may have laid waste to anyone disposed to linger or lie down. Physically, perhaps, only the lucky survived, but mentally, only those with some supernatural tendency toward resilience did.

I am not suggesting that everyone I have seen is over it. They will never be over it; it is a poison, a never-to-be-resolved burning from within. I am saying only that I still cannot see it. They keep it hidden.

Now and again, it's true, there has been a man in his thirties, forties, or even fifties, hardened and muscular, somber, with a lifelessness in his eyes and something very close to the edge of anger—some harshness, something you know instinctively to veer away from and not provoke. In those moments, I confess, I can't help but wonder—*Was he one of the killers?*

It is hard to think of many things worse than judging someone as such, with no evidence. But there had to have been tens of thousands of them. Maybe hundreds of thousands.

That night, Amini Ngabonziza, the student coordinator of the writing club, comes to join us for dinner: broiled tilapia, carrots, potatoes. We sit and watch the street life and talk about writing and education. Amini's hope, like that of nearly every young person we meet, is to come to the United States for graduate work—to receive a visa through the State Department's lottery—but first he has some business to take care of in Rwanda; since the time of the genocide, when he was eight (his birthday, in fact, falls on April 7, the day after the anniversary of President Habyarimana's assassination), Amini has been the head of his household, and still considers himself responsible for seeing that his three siblings receive their education, too.

But after that, he says—he's coming up on his eighteenth year of raising his two younger brothers—after that, he wants to come to the United States and study writing. Not business administration, not agriculture, not political science or banking or medicine or law, but literature, and it is with a kind of thrill and horror both that Terry and I listen to him describe that goal, his need to write. He speaks with the calm clarity that the deepest passion affords—not the adrenaline surge of sudden love, but the deeper, quieter core.

The late afternoon street busy-ness, cast in its splendid butter-yellow light, wanes slowly into the dusk and then true darkness as we visit further and deeper about the artist's sensibilities, and the role of stories in culture and history. All the old verities come tumbling out as if from a vent, a vertical rift, upwelling, brimming orange-gold in the night: the idea that a writer can influence the course of the future, that he or she can say certain things without ever speaking the precise words—that images and stories can touch people's hearts and change the course of their lives. We talk about metaphors, and about morality, and then, of course—where all such late-night conversations converge—spirituality. We talk as if Terry and I are young again ourselves, twenty-somethings, back when such ideas contained not only their own considerable power but also the intoxicating luster of newness: the lava still cooling, cast firm but still warm. And us running through the night across it with the reckless faith that it would hold.

There at our little table—Amini sipping Coke from a straw, Terry and I nursing a second Primus, or maybe a third—our new friend speaks of being unable to *not* write—of writing six, eight, ten pages a night—and though this is not a terribly flattering thing to acknowledge about myself, in that moment, it amazes and confounds me that nothing, not even war, not even genocide—not even hell—can vanquish the artist's spirit, and the desire of a pure young heart to do great good in the world. There is a belief in Amini that words matter, and that actions matter, despite what might seem in Rwanda like overwhelming evidence to the contrary. That good is stronger than evil, love stronger than hate, and that maybe the verdict is still out on the strange and lonely experiment of humanity.

Before he leaves—somehow, it has gotten late—he asks if it would be all right for him to invite to the workshop an elderly professor of his, one who has been singlehandedly championing creative writing among the students, though the professor—François Ntaganda—is not a writing instructor, nor even technically a full professor. Amini says that the professor wishes that American writing instructors could come give lessons not only to the students, but to the teachers—to teach them how to teach. It's evident that he's given it a lot of thought.

"Sure," we tell Amini. "Please invite him. We'd love to have him."

That night, down on the flat streets of Butare, after Amini has left, Terry and I both understand that the slope of the mountain is now right before us—that finally the pitch cants steeply, perhaps impossibly, upward. But in the darkness we cannot see it.

*   *   *

The next morning, when we walk into class, I am as nervous as I have ever been as a teacher. We've only got two days with them, and have organized a variety of writing exercises, mini-lectures, readings, and the like, but while the idea of the genocide as subject matter is on our minds—how can it not be?—something prevents us from naming the elephant. Our job is to talk about *writing*, we tell ourselves, to go over techniques that will help them engage with any topic. "Show don't tell," be careful with adverbs, that kind of thing. There is that, and there is the fact that Terry has been told that there are some political leaders here who do not want survivors to be writing about what happened.

We're delighted, though, to see that Elizabeth has made it to class—since we last saw her, she has found a coworker to take her shifts the next day. (She often works seven days straight at the memorial—I do not want to consider the stress or potential for burnout of such a schedule, and of such work.) She took a bus up to Kigali, then down toward Butare, where she checked in late with her sister and brother-in-law, who teach at a large orphanage about a half hour north of the city. At three a.m. she arose and walked out to the main road, almost an hour away, to catch a slow bus into Butare; we find her sitting in the front row, dressed immaculately, looking once again like a supermodel. Terry and I are both in awe.

To begin the class, we ask them to tell us a little about themselves—the basics, their names and where they're from, and what they hope to get out of our time together. No one responds; instead they all sit there, looking like maybe they're in the wrong room, but too polite to get up and walk out. Finally one of them raises his hand and says—not unkindly, but with no room for negotiation, either—that they want to know who *we* are first. They want to know who we are and, he suggests, what we think we have to offer. *It's only fair*, he seems to be saying. *You go first*.

A tad humbled, but maybe just this side of humiliated, we begin.

"In our country, the government does not always agree with us, or like what we have to say," Terry says. She speaks of her family's history, how eight of the nine women in her immediate family have developed cancer; of how, as a child, riding with her relatives in the Utah desert, she witnessed the nighttime flash of atomic testing, saw and felt the snowlike ash drifting down on her. She tells them of her numerous arrests, her acts of civil disobedience, of resistance, all the while humbly acknowledging how incredibly easy we have it in the United States: how, for all our country's failings, we do have the right of protest, dissent, free speech.

I share my own stories of resistance, which, though they seemed troublesome at the time—death threats, steady scapegoating, vilification in the local small-town newspaper, fire departments refusing to fight wildfires next to my home, car bombings and pipe bombings, all thanks to a few decades' worth of environmental activism—really, at the end of the day, sound like a blessed life indeed by comparison.

I try to explain what it was I was advocating for—big free wild country, and the social right to be able to speak up in one's community for one's values without being persecuted— and I can barely get the words out, I feel like a clay man. It is only with great professional effort that I can push on and pretend that in the face of their experience I have anything to offer them at all: that I am not a fraud, not a tourist.

The students' faces are inscrutable. They do not seem impressed by what they have just heard—but thankfully, neither can I detect any scorn. Impassivity, mostly, with perhaps the faintest trace of confusion showing through. But the contract has been struck, a deal is a deal, and they begin identifying themselves and explaining what they hope to get from the workshop. The most common response is that they want nuts-and-bolts skills—technical assistance. Many of them are like a young man named Cairo, who—as Amini did last night—mentions having work put aside in drawers, never to be seen. They keep writing, because they're writers—the words and stories come spooling out of them—but they don't know what to do next; the drawers become filled, as do previously empty shoeboxes, and finally the cupboards fill, too, not with food but with stories.

One young man speaks candidly of the most lofty of ambitions—"to influence public policy." Another wishes to write a play that will change Africa; another, a grand novel. One wants to be as commercially successful as J.K. Rowling. Another, Alexandre, declares his goal to be "influencing humanitarian issues."

Of the forty or so students in the class, only four are women; one of those is the non-university student, our recently invited Elizabeth. There's a fifth, actually—my daughter Lowry is sitting up at the front, on the other side of the room, eager to hear Terry speak but having received assurances that we will not call upon her. But no sooner have we finished our introductions and begun what I consider the formal process of teaching, the opening up of the toolkits, than one of the students raises his hand and asks who the student is in front, the one who didn't introduce herself. He doesn't say *the white one*, but by the murmured assent, the nods of recognition, we realize they've all noticed her presence. Who's the young woman front left, the pale one, the one with the cornrow braids? I have to laugh out loud—I had thought that because she was quiet, she was invisible. How clueless can I be?

I explain that she's my daughter, and is interested in sitting in and listening, but that I had promised her she wouldn't have to volunteer answers—and I laugh again, and consider the issue resolved—*Let's teach*—but the students are shaking their heads *No, no, everyone has to respond*. It's like a little stalemate, a little mutiny, straight out of the gate, but Lowry saves me by standing up and announcing herself, explaining that she's still in the tenth grade, and is rooming with Terry on this trip. That she is here to learn about their country.

The students relax. Now we can begin.

What do we bring, what do we take back? As if opening a dusty chest, I pull out all the old tropes. *There are only two stories in the world—A man goes on a journey, or A stranger rides into town*. The classic short-story form is elegant, I tell them, with a beginning, middle, and end, and by the last page, something has changed—some greater understanding has been achieved, some conflict has been resolved.

It's old, old stuff, but they're listening carefully: more than carefully. They're listening, if I may mix metaphors, with a ravenous hunger, as if hearing not simple verities or fundamentals but instead the great and complicated secrets that will allow them to bring those sheafs and reams of wrought poems and stories and essays and plays out into the light.

What are they really missing, though? The soil is rich—almost too rich—and the seeds have been planted. There is plenty of yearning, plenty of drive and desire; what one thing yet remains lacking?

As best as Terry and I can tell, it's the absence of a publishing venue, and a publishing tradition, in Rwanda. Historically—beginning with the Twa pygmies, the ancestral forest people who now represent less than one percent of the population—Rwanda's storytellers have followed an oral rather than written tradition. It seems an obvious prescription, then, to find a way to bring the stories out: to develop a publishing network in Rwanda, or to develop and export the stories to countries (such as the United States) where that network—though diminishing—still exists.

The internet, of course, would seem to be a third option, but Terry and I are too resolutely old school to be entirely comfortable with that. The place and time we come from is one in which stories are printed on the skin of trees, cloaked and wrapped in a husk, and able to be used as paperweights. Dense and real things, to be held in both hands rather than existing on a cloud.

Terry and I are still lecturing away, at this point, but our minds are working now beneath the surface. It would be very easy to form a small ad hoc consortium of American literary quarterlies that would commit to publishing a sampling of Rwandan writers; it would not be impossible to secure a grant to publish an anthology of young Rwandan writers, who will one day—maybe forty or fifty years from now—be the last of those remaining from the time that has begun to be referred to in Rwanda simply as Before. It might even be possible to secure a grant to help start a literary journal in Rwanda—something like the *Paris Review* was in the 1950s. Call it the *Rwanda Review*. Anything is possible.

Terry's and my teaching styles are about as different as can be, and we like it that way. The more she leans toward the emotive—lighting candles in the classroom, and speaking of spirit—the harder I lean, I've noticed, toward discussions of passive-versus-active voice, and avoidance of adverbs. She and I have talked beforehand about the genocide question, and about the counsel we've received from friends in Rwanda who've agreed with our instincts to wait for the students to bring it up first, if they choose to bring it up at all—for if by some slim chance it is buried finally at some safe distance within them, what an awkward cruelty it would be for us to dig down through that scar tissue to exhume it. Still, we know, or suspect, that it is not beneath scar tissue. Surely there can be no covering dense enough to bury it other than the stoneweight of deep geological time.

Terry—bolder than I—has sought to begin making a place for a discussion of the inevitable. She reads the class a quote by J.M. Coetzee: "Without truth, no matter how hard, no healing can proceed." She watches them closely, but they do not take the bait: if there are any deep internal salvos of recognition, we cannot discern them. There remains only that untouchable inscrutability, the perfect stillness which, to a Westerner, seems like a kind of retreat.

The further we go, the hotter it gets. Terry's talking about one of the times she was in jail, in Wyoming, and found a collection of nature essays by another western writer, a friend, in a box of books in her cell. That book kept her company through a dark night, she tells them. Books matter, she's saying. Don't give up. Don't keep your work in your bottom drawer forever.

We open the door, we crack all the windows, but still the heat rises and spreads and pools. A trickle of sweat rolls down my spine, top to bottom, straight as a surgeon's incision. Are we pushing, are we doing something wrong? Are we trafficking in gratuitous after-the-fact sensationalism when the kindest and perhaps healthiest thing would be peace and silence—lack of conflict—at any cost?

I don't mean to be beating myself up so much. We're doing the best we can; we're teaching away, dispensing a compressed version of half a century's experience in an afternoon. That's not nothing, it's not even close to nothing, and the students are engaged and asking questions. But this, too, might be part of the invisible and not-entirely-comfortable thing that is building up between us and them: the depth of their need, coupled with the realization, from the very beginning—from before we spoke our first word—that we will be going away. How can such foreknowledge bring anything other than a kind of franticness, an intellectual clutching, on both our parts? *We have only two days together. We have to make them count.*

And already we have managed to lose some of that precious time. During our introductions, the students were still drifting in at a leisurely pace, arriving in a fashion that in our country would be called late, but which I've been told is common here—Rwanda-time. Many of the out-of-the-way places I've been to have a variation on this phrasing—Yaak-time, Alaskan-time, Indian-time—but I have to say, nowhere does time's structure and governance seem less present, or less confining, than in Rwanda. Last night, Amini arrived at the café two and a half hours "late"; this morning, despite our best intentions, we ourselves (with him accompanying us) were a not-so-cool twenty minutes tardy.

In this vein, then, it is Rwanda-normal when a natty older gentleman enters in a navy blazer and with graying hair cut short, his eyes bright behind silver glasses. He has a broad smile and a confident bearing, and Amini introduces him to us as none other than Professor François—the godfather of the writing club.

He's between classes, so he doesn't have long to stay. He's just come to check us out, I think, and to offer his support. For one of our writing exercises, Terry has brought a gleaming fist-sized quartz crystal with her from Utah, and she's passing it around, asking the students to write short descriptions of it: what it looks like, what it makes them think about, how it makes them feel—anything. When we ask them to share what they've written (everything in our workshop will have to be read aloud; there is no access to photocopying), some of them volunteer with a dutifulness that pleases and surprises me, given the natural reserve and reticence we've witnessed—and it is a pleasure also to watch the students loosen, as if unfolding, as they read: to reach that point in each of them where the language and the story rises with a momentum sufficient to transcend self-consciousness.

There is very little teaching or coaching involved in this. That process, in which the ephemeral twists of the heart find their footing upon the relatively firmer substrate of language, sound, and image, stepping from one dry stone to the next, really requires nothing more from us than encouragement. We are standing on the far side of the river, showing them that it can be crossed.

Not all of them volunteer to read. But of those who do, each, it seems, sees the quartz crystal differently. One, who has worked in construction, writes of it as a building material, able to be used in floors and countertops; another, mesmerized, speaks of wanting to hold it forever, and not share it. One is reminded of the fire that birthed the crystal; another is reminded of cool running water. One speaks of how the stone reminds him of his beloved, reading in a rhyme that is somehow not quite hip-hop but carries that infectious, pulsing enthusiasm, so much so that by the time he finishes, the class—no longer reserved—is hooting and cheering, calling out like Congregationalists at a sermon and pressing their palms upward, over their heads—the Rwandan equivalent, I realize, of a standing ovation. And best of all, it is the professor who's leading it, grinning from ear to ear, his brilliant teeth looking ghostly in the dim corner, with his face so very dark. Nothing but teeth, nothing but joy. Where the heck does it come from?

The student, Cairo, the one who like Amini has work packed away in drawers, is modest and humble, but thrilled. He walks back to his seat with a bounce in his step, a sweet kind of almost-secret jive—as if he has just risked almost everything, and has gotten away with it.

The professor—with almost forty years of experience—then does something very smart, very professional. He does not know us from Adam, but he knows Americans, knows the world, and knows too, first and foremost, Rwanda. And so when he stands up—still beaming, so obviously filled with pride in his young students, the face and hope of Rwandan arts and letters—he uses the momentum of the reading to put us on the hook. It's what reporters seek to do to politicians— getting them to answer the hard question on the record—and the impeccability of his timing signifies precisely, I think, the depths of his hunger.

"Look," he says, grinning that laughing-skull grin, spreading his arms wide to include all of us in the phenomenon we've just shared and experienced, "it's easy to come here as Americans and get my students all riled up and excited—but I want to know, are you going to abandon them? Or are you committed to them? What will happen to them when you go away?"

I don't resent it; on the contrary, I admire it. It says much about his heart, his passion, and the generosity of his hopes for the thing he loves—these young people, these survivors—that he would stand up and voice his concerns.

Which isn't to say he *needed* to put us on the hook, exactly. We weren't going to walk away and abandon their artistic hopes. We weren't here seventeen years ago, but that embarrassment, that guilty shame, whatever you want to call it, certainly does not permit us now to raise hopes and then slide away—nor does, I like to believe, our normal moral bearing.

But the professor doesn't know any of that. He only knows what he has seen in the past, and he only knows what he loves.

"There is a culture in Rwanda—in Africa," the professor is saying, "of having to take what is offered, when it is offered, but of not being able to get the best, nor of being able to participate as equal partners in the exchanges. We are hungry," the professor is saying, and he is not talking about food. "How wonderful it would be if you two could help these writers."

Terry and I have already been passing each other short

notes between exchanges with the class; we're ahead of the professor, trying to figure out the same thing. What kind of person could, upon encouraging the most damaged of hearts to open, then turn and walk away? That is not the kind of person I want to be.

Terry looks him straight in the eyes. The professor is still standing, his arms still outspread, hands outstretched, and his mouth is still spread wide in a grin, but he is not smiling. He is waiting.

"We hear you, Professor," she says, "and we will honor your request. We will return."

He blinks, studying us intently—for a second, it seems to me that he is almost off-balance—and then something comes into him, and his grin relaxes once more into a true smile. His face is that of a man who, having examined a thing very carefully, has assured himself finally that he is seeing it clearly, and that it is indeed what he wishes it to be. He nods, grinning now like a kid, and sits his lanky self down, but then—having gotten what he came for—rises again and tells us good-bye and thank you, tells the students good-bye—they say good-bye to him in turn, their respect for him is complete—and he is off to his next class. He seems to me like a man who is aware of two seemingly paradoxical facts, either or both of which are not always grasped by others: first, that we are all extraordinarily tiny in the world, specks or motes so insignificant as to essentially be as invisible as we are momentary—and second, that despite this insignificance, this diminution, we are, and he is, nonetheless immersed squarely in the matrix of history and keenly aware of its movements.

That's a lot to infer, a lot to intuit, a lot to maybe just be making up out of thin air and the invisibility of spirit—the deeply felt, the unspoken—but that's how it seems to me. Before he goes we make plans for the professor to join us for dinner; we have more questions for him than can ever be answered.

Our next exercise for the students is a short piece about place: we ask them to tell us about where they come from. Terry's and my home in the American West is heavily influenced by the open spaces and the keenly felt physicality of the landscape, which braids itself into our writing in the same manner in which characters come and go, exerting their own singular moods and influences; we hunker down and work on our own versions of the assignment, and for ten precious minutes or so, the room fills slowly and steadily with the ineffable elixir of art being created. That sweet silent accumulation of labor that to me is every bit as distinctive as the industrial goings-on in any factory or warehouse.

As we write I think of how several of the students have mentioned that Rwanda has made a conscious effort to promote the study of science and technology almost exclusively; as of next year, apparently, the National University will stop offering liberal-arts classes. This calculated, systematic devaluation of the arts and humanities cannot make the students in this particular classroom feel very good about their government—although it's true that almost all artists, by temperament, inhabit to some degree the peripheries of their society. But while I can understand how a country in a desperate struggle to rebuild would seek to pool its very limited resources in pursuit of the most likely arc of the world's economic future—which, almost anyone would agree, will surely involve science and technology—it feels like a huge mistake to not find some way, even with moral support alone, to acknowledge the importance that stories and storytellers can have in helping shape the foundation of a place. Call me biased, but that's what I believe.

Working there in the classroom, all forty-seven of our pens scratching paper—not a laptop opened anywhere, nor even present, though my sense is that surely some of those here must own them—they're university students, the nation's intellectual leaders!—there is a strange mix of the unified and the isolate. That we are all connected, and even more so through the shared focus of our momentary artistic endeavor, cannot be argued; but it is equally true that within the spheres and cells of our beings we possess moments and memories of exceptional singularity. There are swirls and currents of the mysterious in each of us, and in the near-silence of those ten focused minutes, the room fills with those currents' coils and ribbons: mysteries that are barely transferable sharing space with the deeply common, the deeply shared.

Where do I fit in? Though I will not read my exercise aloud—our time is far too valuable, in far too short supply to be squandered on the indulgence of me talking about myself—I include my effort here, if for no other reason than to prove how alien, how privileged, my own life is, how precious and pretty. And yet here we all are, working together, momentarily common, despite our uncommonality.

Home is always the first thing I hear in the morning—the bray of a wild goose in spring, the cold winds of October, tiny leaves gusting against the window—home is the first thing

I see when I open my eyes in the morning. Whether the day will be foggy or clear, sunny or snowy. Home is where I have the leisure of thinking, upon awakening, whatever I want to think. Home is where I lie down the night before closing my eyes and going to sleep.

I'm very embarrassed to say that when the students stand and read, there are even fewer echoes of the above than I expected. I'm a little puzzled, and find myself wondering if we didn't communicate the assignment clearly. We had explicitly asked for specificity and detail—the scents and sounds of home, the colors and tastes and textures—but as each student rises and reads, the stories are all about family—sisters, brothers, mothers, fathers, aunts, and uncles, whether still living or in memory now. (There is still no mention of the genocide, but anyone and everyone can sense that we are edging closer to it; whether we're being pushed by some force behind us or pulled, summoned, by the central gravity of the thing itself, I do not think anyone could say.) Some of the responses mention the writer's church, but for the most part—overwhelmingly—their definition of home is family. We listen, and provide constructive criticism—parsing out certain individual sentences on the blackboard, to deconstruct and brag upon, when they work; showing how deftly and gratefully one sentence can shoulder and carry such a disproportionate amount of weight in a story, how it can perform so much more than its fair share of the work that needs to be done—but Terry and I remain perplexed by the absence of writing about the verdant mountains, the glowing volcanoes, the scent of the charcoal fires. It is not until much later that night that, back at the hotel, we figure it out: they are refugees. There is no one their age in Rwanda whose childhood was not defined by flight and the absence of place. That they have settled in at the university now, and are living a life of the mind, does not mean that they are not still refugees; thinking about it (which I do not want to do), I fear that to some extent they will be refugees of one sort or another for the rest of their natural days.

Philip Gourevitch, in his book *We Wish to Inform You That Tomorrow We Will Be Killed With Our Families*, muses about why Rwanda has not yet produced great art—or much art of any kind at all—from its darkest horrors, whereas survivors of experiences like the Holocaust have. I think one answer would be to be patient; these students were just babies back then, and are in some instances only a few months or years done with being teenagers now. Wait, and encourage it, and it will come; it cannot be kept below forever.

Maybe we tend to see only what we are looking for, but looking out at the students, never have I seen such hungry, expectant faces; never, as a teacher, have I seen students listening so intently to each word, each idea. That part, I am sure, is not imagined. The thing I am less certain about—the thing I think I am seeing, the thing for which I have been keeping an eye out, the thing I hope I am *not* seeing, is the first true signs of what looks to my untrained eye like depression.

If that is the name for it—the flagging of focus, the distraction, the stillness, the sad and distant gaze out the window—then it is finally here, and why should it not be? Why should it not be everywhere?

What are the statistics in my country—that perhaps as many as one in five Americans are affected by mental illness?

Visiting Rwanda the year after the genocide—when there were still sporadic killings, echo-killings, going on, Tutsis' revenge against Hutus and Hutus still killing Tutsis—Gourevitch wrote of witnessing widespread depression and alcoholism. As I've said, I have not seen it; I am not saying it is absent, only that I have not seen it, and I have been looking. Over the last seventeen years, surely the pressure on the irredeemably depressed has been monumental: surely one by one and then hundred by hundred they have fallen by the wayside and lie sleeping now forever in the same red gardens and fields as those who were killed in 1994 by bullet or machete or club or stone. There are so many different ways to die, inside and out, and so very few of them are peaceful. The rest, as I've said, the ones who remain, are the resilient.

But these students—these artists, these writers—I worry that they are not disposed toward resiliency. I worry that the nature of their artistic temperament puts them a little further out from the comfort of clan or society, all the more distant from the herd or the pack. I do not even know these young people, but I am worried for them, more so than I am for even the little children we've seen scampering barefooted through the mud and gravel streets, possessing nothing, only an exuberance, a brilliance, which in our country might be termed irrational. I am worried for the writers.

Later that night, when I'm commenting to Terry about the way these strange waves of stillness and unease—what looks like sorrow, and deep silences—passed over the students from time to time, she will say that yes, maybe it is depression, but it could also be a sort of learned reticence about sharing too much, in a society where the consequences can be so high. Or it could be something even more basic: the lingering discomfort, lingering confusion, of Hutus and Tutsis being in the same room.

I can't believe my own dimwittedness—the way I have once again looked right at a thing, at a room, and failed to see the obvious. Of course: the general demographics dictate that roughly three-quarters of the students will be Hutu, and the remainder—roughly—Tutsi. The situation might not be as bad as it would be were they all older—surely there are no killers among them, on either side (were they seated next to each other, or self-segregated? I have no idea)—but still, there's got to be a tension, if not a full-on distrust. They should be free to focus on acquiring a depth of immersion in each story; instead, they must contend with such lateral matters as *I wonder if the parents of the man sitting next to me killed my family.*

They're so sweet. They listen to us so carefully, if not yet to each other. At one point I have to almost scold them about this; it may just be a cultural thing, but they sometimes whisper to one another when someone else is reading. It may be that there's just not yet a culture of full support for the workshop model here. I think they still feel isolated.

For us, though, there is utter respect. It reminds me, in some way, of something I've heard often about the genocide: so many of those killed, it's reported, went down without a struggle or a sound. The killers have testified that it was easier work than killing cattle or even goats. Gourevitch writes of several survivors who seemed to have escaped death simply because they put up a struggle.

I know this is a strange comparison to make, but imagine, please, my discomfort: the challenges and fears and frustrations of writing about evil and its seemingly irrevocable aftermath. Even something as simple as mentioning this much-reported observation—that many Tutsis, for whatever reasons (fatigue, malnutrition, shock) died quietly—can freight the writer with guilt, fearful that a reader might misunderstand and inquire, What, are you saying that those who died could have saved themselves, if only they'd fought back?

Not in the least. The RPF fought like hell, defeating time and again much larger forces. But the passivity of death before the rolling and total wave of the genocide—in every village, on every hilltop, in every field—comes up at least briefly in nearly every book about that time; and what I can't help but wonder, in reading such accounts, is to what extent the chronic belittling of Tutsis, the cultural belief that Tutsis were in fact "cockroaches," helped engineer this docility. Generations of hate radio had to have worn down the esteem of a proud minority, and the cumulative effects of all the previous genocides had to have had some kind of profound and ultimately debilitating effect upon them as well—until perhaps at some point, not just among Hutus, but even among certain Tutsis, the unthinkable became no longer unthinkable but instead somehow perversely authenticated by repetition. The idea gains validation merely by surviving across such a distance of time: Tutsis were cockroaches, and Hutus should kill cockroaches.

I can't imagine anyone here still feels that way, if they ever

did—surely the fever of the brainwashing has passed, along
with the quickness toward hatred. When I look out at them,
I tell myself that these are simply young people who are eager
to write.

It's a short class, this first afternoon—three hours will pass
like the blink of an eye—and the surprises just keep coming.
It's been nearly a year since I've taught with Terry, and while
I remember her calm yet mysterious ways—the aforementioned
candles, her personal check-ins at the end of each discussion,
her reverence for all life—I often forget, despite having known
her for over twenty years, how fierce and unyielding she can be.
I'm reminded of it yet again when, as the afternoon draws to a
close, she reiterates that she wants to hear one of the women in
the class read. She's mentioned it once already—there were no
takers—but after announcing her wish a second time, she just
stands there, waiting. Arms crossed. Letting the pressure build.

I'm not comfortable with conflict. I find that I fight
too often, and may well be too quick to fight—in physical
fights, I used to go straight to the biggest guy in the room,
as if to go ahead and get it over with—but I'm still not
comfortable doing it. Standing next to Terry in that increas-
ingly awkward silence, I'm reminded again of how much
I dislike confrontation, how much I crave the serene. It
seems to me that it's not the forty-one young men who are
shouldering the pressure filling up the room, but rather, the
four women, and my overwhelming instinct is to back off—
hasn't it already required enough of their courage just to sign
up for the club, and to show up? Why make it even harder

and more unpleasant for them? Why not trust them to come forward only when they are ready, and not before?

The women—two in the front, one in the middle, one in the back—look deer-in-headlights petrified. I cut a glance to Elizabeth—durable, beautiful Elizabeth with her practice in social situations, speaking all day, every day, to passing-through strangers at the memorials—but she looks no more ready or willing than the other three. I'm almost about to make a request of her, to get me out of my discomfort; I'm just about to give her that look, that silent ask. Instead, I lean over to Terry and whisper, *How about if we just say that we want a woman to read before class is over?*

Terry's so pissed at my suggestion that she won't even look at me. *No*, she says, *we're not going to do anything until a woman reads. We have the time.* Her penetrating gaze moves from one woman to the next, to the next, to the next: summoning them all, and, I have to say it, communicating something to which I am not privy. I don't understand why, if she wants to advocate for these women, and they don't yet want to speak—are not yet ready to speak—she is trying to force them to. I am not seeing it clearly. I can see that there is something between her gaze and theirs—it's a real thing, you can feel it; they are watching her, even as they are steadfastly refusing to say yes—but I have no idea as to the nature of it.

As a result, no one is more surprised than me when the tiny woman seated at the very back stands up as if levitated, announces that her name is Anne-Marie, and begins to read.

You know that feeling when, while encountering a great story—when you are first in the thrall of what you are hearing or reading—you begin to make the transition from hope for its promise to full faith? That magical lift you get when you first understand that the excellence you are experiencing is going to be sustained and even enhanced, all the way through? A beautiful stillness enters the room, in such readings, and this is what Anne-Marie's is like; and though her voice is quiet in the beginning, it gathers strength as she realizes the spell she is casting. When she finishes, she looks up at Terry, altered, no longer shy or hesitant. If ever she was.

Later on, I will confess my moment of weakness to Terry— how I couldn't believe what a hardass she was being, how uncomfortable it seemed like she was willing to make the four women in order to elicit a reading—but Terry will shake her head and say that it wasn't about that at all, that she was only letting them know that she was making a safe place for them, and that she would hold it there; that they were waiting to see if she would be able to hold it.

I was pretty oblivious to this at the time, needless to say. I was looking right at it without seeing it or understanding it.

At the end of class that first day, we pass out the books we've been schlepping, a couple hundred pounds' worth—far more books than there are students, so that we each give each student two books, asking that they pass one on to someone else. Two writers handing out two books: suddenly they're each holding four books, the covers bright and the pages new-smelling, and as Terry and I move up and down the aisle, the combination of joy and stunned good fortune—the disbelief with which they receive our tiny gifts—is like a caricature of a writer's dream.

It's not just about the monetary value of the gift, though you can see in their faces that incredulity also—that nearly a hundred bucks' worth of books (according to the cover prices, at least; the production cost of each one is somewhere between one and two dollars) are being dropped on them. There is real pleasure there. And I have to say, that part— their pleasure, and the pleasure and pride it gives me to be able to make this gift—causes me to feel a little bit of that icky feeling, a little of the guilty liberal's gag reflex at this unambiguous demonstration of the disparity between the inexplicable affluence I possess and the economic realities here. I'm not rich, in the United States—many years, my family's income hovers just barely above the cut-off level for the free school-lunch programs—but I am nonetheless spectacularly, inordinately affluent. I have managed to bring my wife and youngest daughter with me to Rwanda; it is likely that most of the young people in this room will, despite their desires, never see the shores of my country.

So there's a little bit of that. I get to be the generous white big shot, doling out things so common to me as to be taken for granted, yet so cherished by the men and women here. But what makes the whole experience so dreamy, despite the not-so-terrible discomfort of my quasi-obscene affluence, is the realization that the students see these books as a gateway to another world. Valuable for the ideas within, for the beauty of the language and the imagery and the rhythms. I have to say, I've never experienced anything quite like it.

I want to say it one more time: I am not entirely comfortable, not at all, with the America-desire they each and all possess. I know how important, even necessary, it can be to have a dream, a vision of a more idealized place; although there is a part of me that is made apoplectic with rage at how corrupt America has become, how soulless and selfish and short-sighted and isolated—how *spoiled*—there is also a part I suppose I will never be able to shed entirely: the last remnants of pride, or something like pride. The memory that yes, across time, we have done some very good things as well as some very bad. I don't regret or doubt my criticism of our republic-in-freefall— not in the least—but I'm keenly aware, again, of how ungrateful I would sound, harping too much on it. It's evident that the students in Amini's writing club benefit from believing in America as a shining beacon on a hill, and in our books as bits of that beacon; they perceive it as a place where, among other things, writers can actually get their writing published.

And look, this is their truth; is not their distant perspective more accurate, today at least, than my own embittered one?

As if a church service has ended, we stand at the door and shake hands with each of the students as they file out, their arms filled with our gifts. One asks if he can visit with Terry in private, and they step outside into the late-day sun, where I see him addressing her, at length, with great seriousness and intensity, while she listens with deep concern and focus: wanting, I can tell, to be sure she is hearing and understanding him correctly. When they part, she looks a little worried, but also a little relieved, as if she now possesses some knowledge she almost wishes she didn't have.

"He says we're going too soft on them," she tells me, on the walk back to the Ibis. He was almost chastising her, she says, beseeching her: *Give us encouragement to put our lives on the line with what we write.*

Terry told him that we are being cautious; that we are visitors.

"No," he said. "You are writers."

I knew that what she'd heard was heavy, but I didn't know it was that heavy. And as she tells me about it, I understand also that even though it wasn't exactly what she and I wanted to hear, in another way it kind of was.

He wasn't just asking her to talk about the elephant in the room; he was pretty much asking us to help him go track one down and kill it with nothing more than stone-age spears. Words on paper tablets, and small meetings, small gatherings of like-minded people. All their lives, they've kept their stories bottled up; now they are at the age when such hesitation starts to seem like a waste.

Sometimes, here in the flat wide waters of middle age, I get a little frantic, and a little pissed off, when I realize that I am drifting, floating, living as if there is indeed a tomorrow, and not as if tomorrow, or even later today, the world I know and love could crack open and a great and all-consuming fire could come roaring up from below. I know what it means to feel like the truth must be confronted. I do believe that these students should write down the stories that they have been keeping hidden and buried—surely they did not survive only to remain forever silent—but I also simply do not have the assurance of any moral authority to support this belief. Maybe my job as a benumbed Westerner is to live more intensely, while their job—having had several lifetimes' worth of intensity—is to rest up and heal, and to sleep.

The student who corralled Terry after class disagrees. We're going to have to make a decision tonight, at dinner. Knowing

Terry, I can already predict what that decision is going to be, and the responsibility of it fills me again with the most awful and unaccustomed kind of moral apprehension.

It may seem that I am making too much of it. It's just forty-five kids in a classroom, lost or drifty artists who may by temperament be disposed to have a tougher time in the world—especially in Africa—than others; it's not like we're debating whether to commit our soldiers, our peacekeeping troops, to save hundreds of thousands of innocent lives. I'm a writer, and a teacher. Teachers teach. I'm here, and in the morning, I'll teach. But I still don't know how to do it.

The professor joins us an hour later, at our outdoor table, where our glass mugs of Primus are effervescing in the lying-down sunlight, spirals of fizz swirling slightly upward. He's very happy to see us, and very happy to have gotten our answer, to know that we will continue to help, will continue to invest in his students even after the workshop is over.

His age is indeterminate; his short hair is graying, as I've said, and there are some lines on his face. Fifty, even nearer to sixty? It's hard to say, not knowing the circumstances of his days, the path he has traveled.

He was educated in the Congo, he tells us—his family fled there from one of the earlier genocides—and it was there in the Congo that he decided to become a teacher, inspired by the example of an uncle. When we ask him how he came to literature—having assumed that, as with most lit people, it had always been his burning passion—we get an answer we didn't expect.

Literature, he says, was his third choice. Science was first, and engineering was second. But back then a literature teacher was needed—French literature, specifically—and thirty, maybe thirty-five years ago, that was the hole, the gap, he was asked and expected to plug. Things have happened since then, big things; the killings have come and gone and somehow again he survived them, and now—despite knowing next to nothing about the teaching of creative writing, though plenty about old novels from France—it may be that he is in the one place where the world most wants and needs him to be. For whatever reason, he finds himself deep into middle age and still blowing the steady breath of the living—the steady breath of a survivor—upon the faint coals and embers of his students.

The professor says that he lost everything at a village called Murambi; that his place is there, with the ghosts. It's yet another memorial now, one that we'll visit tomorrow, after class. It's also in the exact opposite direction of where we'll be going next—up toward Ruhengeri and Virunga National Park, to see the gorillas—but again, it's the least we can do: the least disrespectful thing, so many years later. The professor says that he will ride out there with us. The memorial at Murambi is notable for the fact that the corpses have not yet rotted; they were stacked so deep in the mass graves that there wasn't enough oxygen for decomposition to occur in the bottommost layers of the twenty-foot pits. This was not the only thing that stalled the process; dump trucks of lime were poured over the graves as well.

After the genocide, these bodies were exhumed. Their skin has merely shrunk in around them, like a small coat drawn ever so much tighter, and now they are on display in various rooms, on tables, intact. Most troubling of all is the fact that the bodies are still arranged in the perfect gestures—the perfect agonies—of their last moment of life. You want to avoid going, and yet you do not want to be the person who avoids going.

Dinner arrives, and we eat, and visit more, though not about sad or somber things. Our Rwandan Elizabeth, who has joined us as well, is quiet, and when Terry asks her what she's thinking about, she says she's thinking about how much like a dream it all seems. One day she is going about her job, and the next day—the very same day, actually, but in the next moment—a group of strangers from America arrive, and invite her to come and learn how to pursue her heart's desire, her heart's secret wish.

Later in the evening, we drive Elizabeth back north of town, to where she's staying with her sister and her sister's husband. The dark road is still filled with pedestrians; we drive extra carefully. When we reach the turn-off to the boarding school, the orphanage, where her sister and brother-in-law teach, she says she can walk the rest of the way, that the road is rough and that it is not so far away.

I know it's her home, for the moment, but the darkened town looks sketchy. It's late, and the markets are closed, save for a couple of stucco buildings that look like bars, where plenty of people are still congregated, sitting under yellow light bulbs drinking beers. People are walking up and down the warped and twisted roads—the town is on a hilltop, and there are big stones sticking up in the middle of the road, around which a driver has to navigate, while at the same time trying to avoid the deepest craters—and I find myself unsure if they will receive Elizabeth with the same warmth with which we ourselves were received, earlier in the day. It would be formidable even on foot, but our big SUV should be capable, and we tell Elizabeth that we'd really rather drive her all the way in.

She protests again, and without our realizing it, it's probably one of those cross-cultural-rudeness things at which we Americans are often so adept. It occurs to me that for Elizabeth—shy Elizabeth—to protest a second time, and then, with less vigor, a third, she must really mean it—she would really rather walk the rest of the way. But the rest of us are all caught up in that thing we do, for example, when a check comes at a restaurant: the insistence on one person paying instead of another, or instead of simply splitting the bill. In its worst stages, it can become a kind of bullying.

It's a little like that here. We win the debate, of course, and proceed, the high carriage of the Lexus rising slowly and then pitching downward, rising and falling like a great ship at sea, plowing the troughs and crests of a turbulent ocean. The flow of upstream humanity braids slowly around us, making way for our passage—what important cargo must be inside such a mysterious vehicle, with its tinted windows and unimaginable opulence!—while the headlights pierce the cloudy sky above. Elizabeth seems a little tense, but does not protest any further; the argument has been won, we have imposed our will.

I know it seems silly to be worrying over someone who spent

a hundred days running for her life—if she says it's safe for her to walk the rest of the way, then it must be, for who better can know what safety is than one who has so completely plumbed the depths of danger?—but it's not something our culture is real comfortable with, sending a young woman off into the night on her own. And so with our great tank moving no faster than a slow walk, we pitch carefully over the ruts and around the toothy stones. As is sometimes the case with such efforts, we have projected our fears and discomforts onto the object of our generosity. Little wonder that the recipient then feels in such instances less comforted or valued, rather than more.

It reminds me of how, a little earlier in the drive, I had mentioned to Elizabeth how concerned I am about cell phones: about the only-now-emerging evidence that links the radiation they emit to the growth of tumors in their users. In countries like Israel, where cell phones have been in use longer, the number of cancer cases—particularly in the brain and in the salivary glands, against which the phone rests—has skyrocketed in young people. Cell-phone manufacturers have actually started issuing warnings—in extremely fine print— that identify their products as emitters of radiation, and warn users to not expose themselves to it. No one I've spoken to has ever read or even seen the fine print. It's an epidemic, I told her, a secret, silent, deadly wave, much as cigarettes were, sixty and seventy years ago.

On and on I prattled, just making conversation, while Elizabeth listened politely, without comment. Did she feel I was criticizing her use of cell phones? It's the rap I give my own children, and all young people. It's one of the hidden truths of the world today, one which is in my opinion extraordinarily dangerous, with consequences that may well be irredeemable, unfixable. But at some point in Elizabeth's polite silence I got it, if belatedly: why is the *muzungu*, seventeen years after the season of the machetes, warning me about telephones? *What an utter indulgence*, to even consider worrying about such things—invisible things—that have not happened yet, and which may not ever happen!

I had already gone on for too long by then, of course. The gulf between my country and this one, between my country's neuroses and this country's justified fears, can feel as wide as the ocean itself.

We're driving through a dense fog. If not for the people sitting on the storefront porches sipping their beer, it would look like a ghost town. Elizabeth directs us through a series of left and right turns, the cumulative effects of which are starting to confound; it would have been a long walk. We roll the windows down, and the green damp scent of springtime relaxes us. There are fewer people around now. Mysterious night birds are calling, steam is rising from the road, ground fog drifts gently past us as if we're in a river, and we're driving slowly enough that we can hear each cricket for a long time before we move on to the next one, and the next.

Ahead of us, a giant, ghostly figure appears, looming thirty feet tall or higher: a pale figure in a robe.

"What's that?" I ask Elizabeth—my night vision is not the best, and the fog is not helping matters.

There's just the briefest hesitation on her part as she formulates the most tactful answer: as she tries to parse out what I might and might not know about religion, and not wanting, I think, to sound disrespectful.

"That is Jesus Christ," she says evenly, without judgment.

We're close enough now that we can see all of him in the headlights. There's a big Catholic church in the background, on our left, looking like something from Italy, and a low rock wall on our right. The statue is up on a pedestal, and this Jesus looks different, somehow, from the ones of my youth. He's white, of course, and blue-eyed, but he has a dense black beard, which gives him kind of a burly look, like a northwoods logger. Somehow, he looks a little more formidable.

From out of the fog, just beyond the giant statue of Jesus, a line of very small children appears, walking from right to left. It is ten-thirty in the evening. They are dressed in school uniforms and each is carrying a bucket of water in each hand. They are laughing as they walk, being careful not to slosh any water, and we stop and watch as they pass in front of us, a long procession of them, as if we are stuck at a railroad crossing, waiting on an endless chain of boxcars. Are they finishing classes only now? Are they going back to their dorms, or are they simply completing their chores? After my gaffe with asking who the big guy with the beard was, I tell myself to simply watch—to observe the strange and lovely image of laughing children passing through the middle of the night— and after the last of them has filed past, we turn onto a grassy field. There is no more road, only the faintest bend to the tall green grass, which indicates that maybe, possibly, someone drove this way not so long ago. I drive on, slowly, through the field and through the fog, trusting that if I need to veer left or right, Elizabeth will correct me.

After a while, farther below us, we see the long row of lights that is the school. It appears to be a two-story brick building, and every window is ablaze, though dim and yellow in the fog. It's not so far away, but the little squares of windowlight make it look like a distant village on the other side of a valley. It has to it also the look of a gigantic submarine, out in the middle of nowhere, one which perhaps only surfaces once a year, and which has chosen, on this night, for whatever reason, to appear.

As we draw nearer—Elizabeth directs us farther down the hill, toward the most distant end of the long, barracks-like structure—we see that there is a high protective wall around the school, as might surround a castle; and when we reach the end of the field, where no road whatsoever exists, Elizabeth thanks us and gets out. Almost immediately, she is completely invisible, save for the luminous white of her shirt.

But with the car stopped, we can hear now the most amazing sound: the chorus of all the children singing, each in their room. A unified song, a good-night song, perhaps— the same song coming from every open window, and spreading out through the darkness of the night. It is one of the most beautiful choirs I've ever heard, all the more so for our understanding that it is being sung for no listeners, no audience, though we are fortunate enough to have stumbled up against the edges of it. And all the more strange, too, all the more powerful, for the fact that I picture each child walled off from the others like bees in a honeycomb, slightly separated yet completely together.

Elizabeth, caught in the headlights now, waves good-night, walks up to the heavy wooden gate of the fortress, and knocks twice. The gate opens, and she disappears inside. The singing continues; we sit there for a long time afterward, listening, and feeling every small scar and bruise within us healing, every twist stretching and straightening, every worry-line flattening, every tension soothing.

There is a shape to all stories. The next day, we begin the class as we would almost any other—as if believing that there will not be anything extraordinary lying before us.

And for the first ten or fifteen minutes, that is how it seems the day will be: an interesting and stimulating journey through relatively flat terrain, through techniques and imagery and metaphor, with perhaps a few foothills involved, but nothing extraordinarily strenuous. Our friend the professor is absent— he is teaching another class—but there are new students today, more than there were yesterday, and there's even another young woman among them. We pass out more books to those who did not receive them already, and again they are received like sacrament, with double-handed reverence.

It is as if we are walking with blinders on. And why not, when we have seen so many days like this? If the trail begins to pitch upward slightly, we do not take it a sign of things to come. We do not consider that we might finally, after a long time, have reached the flanks of the volcano.

But despite our best efforts, the classroom lecture will not ignite. It's Terry, finally, who first interrupts our steady progression and says, bluntly, "Yesterday after class one of you came to me and asked us to talk about why you should take political risks."

You have seen things, she says—you have stories to tell about the genocide that some people may wish were kept quiet. Or perhaps the truth of what you see now in Rwanda is a truth the government does not want voiced. "It's easy to be a writer in America," Terry tells them, "even a writer of resistance. We are not going to be killed. But here, as you all know, last summer a journalist was beheaded for writing words against the president."

She doesn't stop there. The students are listening.

"Your risks are far greater than ours," she says. "But what we do share with you, passionately, is a desire to tell the truth of our lives. In this, we can offer you our experience and our encouragement." And then she turns to the student who approached her yesterday.

"Your charge that we have been timid is true," she says. "We respect you. We don't want you to be hurt. But that is not for us to decide. You are here, and we feel your fire. Being a writer in Rwanda demands a different kind of courage."

What happened, she says, must have torn their hearts open—whether they are artists or not has nothing to do with that—and we begin talking about how they must not expect their young hearts to be healed; they may never be healed. You can tell your stories directly or indirectly, we say, but you must tell them. They are too important to remain hidden in a drawer.

A change sweeps over the students as we are saying this. There is an immediate, palpable release—the cap is off the volcano—and suddenly all of them look five to ten years older: still young, but mature, experienced. They look stronger, and less innocent, but also less plagued, perhaps, by the exhausting efforts of inhabiting the safe confines of a certain constricting numbness.

Is it a necessary numbness? What have we authorized, asking them—encouraging them—to come out of it?

The top was going to come off anyway, of course. They would not have invited us here if they had not wanted it to come off. We are ascending now, walking behind them. We can feel the heat beneath the soles of our shoes, can feel the heat at the top of the mountain, can see up ahead the strange corona of firelit gases, brimstone in the air.

We give another brief writing assignment. Ten minutes. If you had only one story left to write in your life, I tell them, what would it be? If there was one thing, one story you wanted to pass on into the future, one story that would not be carried forward otherwise, what would it be?

A silence falls upon the room, and then, slowly, pens begin to scritch. Sentences spool across the pages.

What pours out is amazing. It is for Terry and me as if we have entered another, hidden world, one where there is only excellence, only beauty. It is a world where no instructors are needed, and no instruction, only fire, beautiful, dangerous, destructive fire flowing down the slopes, following nothing more than the brute instinct of gravity. We listen in awe to one tale after another—their one-last-stories, their first stories, here in the new part of their lives, the next part, where they know now what they always suspected, that they have an audience—that the world is waiting, and that the stories must come out.

Anne-Marie, emboldened by the safe space that Terry made for her yesterday, rises and reads two poems, each of which is the equal of some of Mary Oliver's finest work. Cairo reads a poem about lions, leopards, tigers, and men—a parable, an allegory—

that is the equal of W.S. Merwin's, with its economy and native wisdom, and its grip, its grasp, at the end, upon the heart.

Two different stories from other students, written independently, on opposite sides of the room, relate similar events: an oldest brother, who would have been six or seven, responsible for any siblings who managed to survive after the parents were gone; a brother going out into the bush and finding his siblings and caring for them, and the toddlers and infants ultimately passing away without their mothers to nurse them; a six-year-old boy, a seven-year-old boy, carrying the guilt and pain and grief of that failure, that loss, on top of all others.

Tears are rolling down Terry's cheeks as we listen to the stories—as we ascend. I myself am just a half-beat behind her, if I could let just one more crack of light into my heart—could allow it to be shoved open a bit wider, pierced a little more deeply—but looking out at the students' faces, I catch myself and remember that they did not ask us here to watch us cry. It's important for them to see that great writing can move people to tears, but I perceive dimly, and just in time, I think, that it's also important to show them their writing being treated professionally; they still want the nuts-and-bolts, the how-to. And so I shut out the slats of sunlight that are strafing my heart—that have just brushed against it. What good would it do these young people, who have seen so much, to watch both of their instructors cry? How would that help them now?

Instead I pretend to be hard. Not quite as if I hear these sorts of poems and essays every day, but instead as if the task of getting them into the world is too important to waste time on the indulgence of tears.

Traveling on instinct—hoping, believing that what's best is for only one of us to dissolve, not both—I skim past and across my own subterranean chasms, happy, grateful, that Terry, my dearest friend, is having her spirit addressed, tended, illuminated, healed. I try on the persona of ebullient agent or enthusiastic car dealer: as if I am not surprised by this excellence, as if I have even expected it. I might sound patronizing here; I might sound manipulative, presenting to the class a persona other than my true and honest self. But sometimes you catch yourself just in time.

Terry dries her eyes, boards up her broken-open heart with no small degree of reluctance. I can't say how much I love and appreciate her. It's kind of an out-of-body experience, this pretending for their sake not to be heartbroken, but in the first few seconds of inhabiting the role, of stepping forward, I can tell that I have made the right choice.

It is the thing they did not expect. Surely they saw the expression on my face—the tears on their way. But now that I am speaking, alertly, enthusiastically, their faces illuminate. This is the thing they have been waiting for—as much as wanting to be heard, they want to be *good*. And in this out-of-body moment, where I am looking down on myself teaching, I can see myself addressing the students about the specifics of what we have just heard—what works, and why. The alliteration, the pacing, the perfect ratio of what is said versus what is not. I tell them these things, and force myself not to think: to just talk. These students, who have crossed first, have come over the river without even the tips of their feet touching the water. It is more than a little like they have flown.

I occupy the role of cheerleader with the fullest enthusiasm I can, seeing now how they are made young again by their hope and pride. It seems to pass over all of them at once, as with all their shared emotions; as if despite their differences—some Hutus, some Tutsis—they are more deeply connected than we on the outside can ever know. I'll say it: as if they are connected by blood.

Fed by their reinvigoration, I move to the chalkboard and begin diagramming nouns and verbs, subjects and objects: blasphemy, really, for when something works at the highest levels, as their poems and stories do, no deconstruction is necessary; but it's the time-honored thing that workshops offer, and again, for some reason it seems to bring us the full and normal experience of American teaching, secondary and unexceptional though that is compared to what has just transpired. I gesture and chart with the zeal of a barker advertising a weekend Toyota sell-a-thon. I tell them that they are great—that they have written great things—and because it is true, and they know it, they receive the words like water in the desert, like water on a dry garden, drip by drip.

One by one they raise their hands to ask more questions, to offer up their stories. It's electric.

While the enthusiasm is running hot, we segue to the discussion of publishing plans: the brainstorming about how to get these stories, these writings, out to an international audience, which, as Terry notes astutely, can be its own form of protection against whatever political oppression or persecution might come. That's something else we can offer—illumination—

and we begin listing literary journals that we think would be interested in working with them, maybe a loose confederation of magazines around the U.S. and even in other countries that would be interested in committing to a Year of Rwandan Writers—each magazine agreeing to publish three or four pieces as part of a special project, perhaps with an introductory essay by an established writer: an introduction to a new generation of Rwandan writing.

We can find a grant, we tell them, to publish their club's writings in book form as well—an anthology—and it's a shame the professor isn't here today to see their joy at this promise. We don't know where we'll find the grant, but we will; we've told them we will, so we will. We're on the hook, just like the professor wanted.

It might be simplest just to convince one certain lit mag to do a special issue, but our thinking is that the nature of the project calls for a confederation, an alliance, a coalition, to demonstrate the idea that there is not just depth of support for the idea, but breadth. Perhaps in this thinking we are operating from a place in the subconscious, a part of us remembering that there was a time in these young people's history when the thing most needed was this kind of response: not any one country or entity listening, but a whole brigade of them.

"We can look for grants to help you start a literary publication in Rwanda, too," we go on—promises, promises!— "some high-quality quarterly that can represent the best of Rwandan writing." We're picking up on our notes from yesterday, remembering the venerable *Paris Review* again, started in a room no larger than this one, over fifty years ago:

a publication to which every writer in Rwanda, or even Africa, can aspire. Why shouldn't the smallest country in Africa assume the mantle of publishing a region's literature? Of announcing, and making a way for, voices that must be heard? The more we think and talk about it, the more excited we get. Is this some inkling of how it felt to European "discoverers"? The realization that one has stumbled into a land of great riches and resources, so that the exploitative part of the human mind—which is to say, the largest part—begins whirring, seeking to establish and colonize? Maybe. We're not feeling greed—we've come to give, not take—but I can't help but wonder if the excitement isn't a little bit of the same. There are already some well-regarded African journals, of course— *Kwani?*, *Chimurenga*—and things like the Caine Prize, but a journal based in Rwanda seems right, the country seems fertile. The more the better.

Terry writes a timeline on the blackboard. The coming summer will be spent writing, revising, writing, revising. By September they will send us their poems and stories, which we will edit, and then they will revise again. "In revision, things become magic," Terry says. Then we'll publish, distribute the publications, and come back in the summer again. It's that simple. And it's also that hard.

If you stand together, you will be protected, we tell them, and I hope that is the truth. I hope that we are not giving them the exact wrong advice, and the exact wrong encouragement, in the same manner in which children like them were told, seventeen years earlier, to go and hide in the churches. I hope that never again are death lists drawn up, with political leaders and intellectuals occupying the top. Such lists existed in my own state, in extreme northwest Montana, where, during the height of the timber wars and the anti-government militia movement of the late 1990s—around the time of the Oklahoma City bombing—vast stores of weapons were stockpiled, and hate radio broadcasts occurred daily. Those lists were never acted upon, but they existed; their drafters were members of no organized political party or movement, but instead embittered anti-government hermits. Some of them were arrested in the Flathead Valley of Montana, or killed in shoot-outs with federal agents in places like Ruby Ridge, Idaho, and that fever, that clamant, blind hatred, faded as if it had never been anything more than a dream.

Certainly, the stories—the testimonies—these young people will be sharing could draw attention to them as chroniclers. It is this same thing that will protect you, we assure them. If the world is watching and listening—if you are published authors—it makes things safer for you, not more dangerous.

We want to believe this. We do believe this. And they have to write, anyway; they are writers.

One by one, the students raise their hands, then rise to speak. Jean-Bosco tells us that we have opened the gate to making sense of what he does, and that because of this, he is back in the world. Ahvit stands up and says, "Previously, I only knew America as a country that invades other countries. Now I know that you love us." The student who spoke to Terry at the end of the first day rises and, with no small amount of calm resolve, announces, "You have reminded me of the need for me to achieve my duty as an artist, as I first dreamed many years ago."

It's embarrassing, it's overwhelming. I tell myself it's not all about us, but instead, about the vessel of us—the reservoir of hope we offer—and for this reason, it's important not to deflect or dismiss or self-deprecate in the face of their most sincere praise, but instead, to suffer it, absorb it, revel in it. A student named Amcai tells us, "When you have stories such as we have, and you keep them, it is a problem." He shrugs. "We don't want to keep them."

Terry nods, and shares the old African proverb about sticks: "One stick is easily broken, but a bundle of sticks—no." We are asking you to build a community, she says.

Amcai replies with a proverb of his own: "If a child grows up in one day, it's a problem." Again, we're on the hook; we understand that we won't just be able to offer our encouragement and then walk away. The new female student, Carol, rises and says, simply, "I know you love us very much."

The old-school clock on the wall, a clock I remember from my days in elementary school more than forty years ago, indicates that we have scant minutes left. Ahvit has been thinking some things over, and has more to say. "In my dream, we are together," he says, then lowers his head slightly and says that he is ashamed: that he will not deceive us, but that he has nothing he wants to show us yet. "I want to change my neighbors," he says. "I want to change the world."

On and on it goes, an outpouring. "I think this conversation should have started the other workshop," one student says, not unkindly, and then Ahvit has more.

"I would call what happened today a revival, in that it touches the spirit. Frankly speaking, the spirit of writing seemed to be dying in me. But not now."

TOP: *Clothing at the church at Ntarama.*
BOTTOM: *Rebuilding, seventeen years later, north of Kinigi.*
All photos by Lowry Bass.

TOP: *The market in Kinigi.* BOTTOM: *A mosque in Rugerero.*
OPPOSITE: *Rudacyahwa Cairo, poet, National University of Rwanda.*

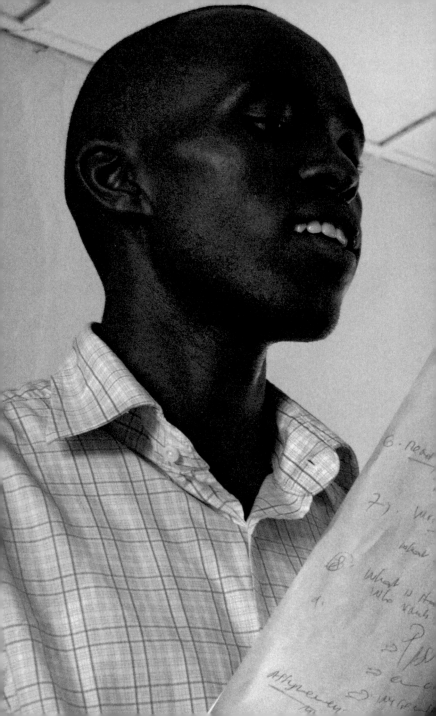

TOP: *The author and mountain gorilla, at Virunga National Park.*
BOTTOM: *Mother gorilla and young.*

We can count the seconds remaining in the day. We are committed to travel to the Murambi memorial, farther south, with Elizabeth and the professor, before turning around and heading back north, all the way up into the mountains on the northern border, to gorilla country. We have overextended ourselves: we want to do everything, help everything, see everything. Terry has purchased a woven basket, and in closing out our time together, she asks that each of us write down on a scrap of paper our great wish for the coming year, and place the slip of paper in the basket; and a year from now, when we meet again, we will open the basket and read aloud the anonymous wishes, to see which ones might have come to be, and in what fashion.

As the basket is being passed around, there is one last comment, and an appropriately self-aware one, I think, after a day of so much raw emotion. A shy young man rises and says what we have all been thinking: that his generation of Rwandans has stories that must come out. "All our blessings to you, indeed," he says generously. "But what if, when you return to America, you tell them that there is a new thing we have discovered in Africa?"

We've overstayed; my Elizabeth and Lowry have arrived with bags from the hotel. François the professor has arrived, too—we shake hands, embrace all the students, distribute the last of our books like missionaries passing out stacks of red Gideon Bibles, and file out onto the lawn to take a group photo.

The students are exuberant, radiant, giddy; they inhabit the spring sunlight with broad grins, hugs, and much animated conversation. It is impossible not to think that a shell has been cracked open for them, an encasement, one they did not want. In our photos, they are leaping, smiling and leaping high, released; and in my own memory, so subject to alterations, adjustments, and amendments, that was how it was: we turned and left even while they were still leaping, still suspended, in flight.

The road to Murambi is a rainslicked slanted mountainside trail, with breathtaking views of the small narrow valley below. Rwanda's mountains seem to surround the village—everywhere you look there is a beautiful green hill, sparkling in the late-day sun, and beyond that, perhaps twenty or more miles farther on, the larger mountains, and the Congo.

As Rwanda's population swells, seemingly unhindered by the cycles of genocide and the chronic advance of AIDS (not all of the orphanages we pass are the result of the 1994 genocide; they are receiving fresh recruits annually, by the tens of thousands), the rural villages are forced to expand ever-higher up the slopes of the mountains, tilling ever-steeper lands, which then wash away in the heavy rains, worsening an already dire problem. (The average farm size in Rwanda is one acre per family—barely more than a large subsistence garden.) This, combined with the deforestation that fuels the $7 billion charcoal industry we observed a bit of earlier, is robbing Rwanda of the foundation it stands on, and its hope for a future—any future—just as surely as any wars, or any blood-borne illness. These latter challenges may or may not be overcome, but in the meantime, hidden not in the hearts of men but visible right before our eyes, the country is washing away. Entrepreneurs, scientists, progressive thinkers, and other revolutionaries are trying desperately to come up with solutions that might buy time, but the rivers will soon be running redder than ever. This is a worldwide problem, of course; Robert Kunzig, in a recent *National Geographic* article, estimated that the rate of soil erosion from plowed fields is ten to a hundred times the rate of soil production. Soil scientist Wes Jackson, of the Land Institute, wrote thirty years ago that "unless this disease is checked, the human race will wilt like any other crop."

We know what crop we will find on the hilltop at Murambi, exhumed from the apoxic lime-pits of the mass graves, and as we approach I find myself caught in another strange emotional triangulation: the stimulation of the workshop; the horror of what we are traveling to see; and the overwhelming beauty of the landscape, like the world's largest hanging garden, with glittering streams and waterfalls clinging to the slopes like bright necklaces. This is the natural abundance that may vanish, sand through the hourglass, but it is not gone yet, it has not yet vanished today.

Yet another triangulated tangle: the dwindling space made evident between betrayals, in which one must choose whether to trust one's instincts, or one's political leaders, or the cores and patterns of history. Yes, the churches were once safe, have always been safe, but are they now? Doesn't everything change? And yes, the mayors and *interahamwe* say to stay put, but what of the wild bird of terror in the heart that says *Flee*

*now, do not even pack, leave the country, abandon your home and all
that you have built?*

All across Rwanda, that first night, families and friends
were having that conversation, with the space of that triangle
constricting so quickly, and so much—the green breath of
life—at stake. Some shrugged and obeyed orders, and lived;
others did the same and died. Some obeyed their hearts and
fled, and survived; others, who followed them, did not. Some
followed the priests into the churches. Almost all of those
were lost. A few survived, if it could be called that, only
because they were not noticed.

Here at Murambi, political leaders asked the Tutsis to walk
to the nearby technical school for safety. Tens of thousands
did so, only to find themselves unprotected; after several days
of scattered attacks, the school was overrun on April 21. The
shooting began at 3:30 a.m. and did not finish until 11. The
big machines were at the ready by then, plowing the deep
trenches and piling the bodies in by the thousands, the rich
soil cut fifteen feet deep. Survivors tried to crawl out, and
to pull out others who were only wounded, but the tractors
kept shoving the dirt over them, and the dump trucks kept
showering them with lime.

Something about the hilltop location—all of beautiful,
rural Rwanda visible, it seems, from up here, and on such a
lovely day—and the demeanor of the young man who will be
guiding us suggests that we will be experiencing a different
sort of memorial. François, the professor, is tense. Surviving is
not the same thing as escaping.

We walk slowly to a mass grave, where our guide explains
the history to us. He glances at my ballcap just as I am

removing it. A moment later he gestures to the compound behind us, just a little farther up the hill: a garrison, with rows and rows of rooms, in which, he tells us, 848 recovered bodies "are sleeping."

He's speaking with extraordinary softness, as if to avoid disturbing them. "Okay," he says. "Now we can start our visit."

Swallows knit the reddening sky above us, darting and swooping as if rapidly casting a great net. The grass in this hilltop field is green and tall and sways in the breeze. The guide says that when the killers came here the Tutsis fought back, but all they had were stones.

Cows are lowing from the fields down below, and, crazy as this sounds, their groans and grunts are different. I grew up in Texas, and have since spent all my days in the ag states of Mississippi, Alabama, and Montana; I've heard cattle all my life. But this evening the bellows of these cows are deeper, longer, and slower—more anguished—than any I have ever heard. While there may well be an explanation—perhaps the grass they have been grazing, which is a more vibrant green than any I've seen, is contorting their ruminants' stomachs in such a way as to produce that ghastly sound—it's nonetheless unsettling. It's a sound from some deeper, buried place, straining to rise and be released; it's as if it's filling the cattle with unbearable torment before being released to the sky.

I will try to pass through these rooms quickly, in my memory. They are in neat rows, as if in a hotel, and the view is sublime; a concrete porch runs the length of the nearest row, from which a viewer's gaze is directed to the red skies of the west.

The first room we enter is called the Babies' Room.

Like no place yet, the air is truly fetid, rather than merely rank or musty; this is the real deal, death still in progress, a singular stench of the sour and the sweet. Under no ordinary circumstances would you enter a room that smells this bad. We follow our guide in slowly. It is an act like swimming: the odor is that dense.

The bodies are so very small. They are all intact, all cloaked in ghostly lime. They are slightly desiccated but they are still fully bodies, with facial features preserved. They would be identifiable by name, if we knew them. Some of them have their arms uplifted in gestures that make it look as if they had been dancing, joyful, rather than in agony. As if ultimately only a hair's-breadth register of difference separates the two conditions in the illuminated hothouses of our brains.

The guide is crying quietly. Has he given this same tour eight hours a day, six days a week, for the last seventeen years? How many tears can the body produce? How many, the heart? I suppose it depends upon the story. I do not want to know any more of this story, but it is his obligation, his calling, to tell us a little more: we who have gotten here so very late.

"It is here we can find the definition of genocide," he says, his voice thicker still. "In the Babies' Room."

Perhaps the worst of it is that these aren't even really the babies, but the children: toddlers. There is another room of infants and newborns, but that door is locked now, because visitors to that room were passing out, collapsing, so that they themselves had to be rescued, carried back out into the light and the living. The bodies of babies who had experienced only the first few hours of life. The first few moments.

Here in the room of the slightly older babies, the skulls

are still so very tiny. Some of them have bullet holes in them. Some of the little skulls are missing their tops. A common testimony is that many parents were forced to kill their own children in order to prevent them from being tortured. Our guide is dabbing his eyes. I don't know what his own story is.

It's the strangest thing. I force myself to study—to behold— each of the little people, but I can't help but be aware of the motion and light and color in the air beyond the stink of the gray-lime lightless body-room. Out on the hillside, in one of those one-acre gardens, a man is swinging a machete, maybe cutting ears of fresh corn; I don't want to look too closely. A little farther down from that, a baby boy is shrieking with laughter as a woman swings him by his arms, around and around. And then from out of that tall grass there emerges another child, a toddler who cannot be more than three years old.

He's very close to us, and very beautiful. The lying-down sun casts a gold glow on his face. He watches us, entranced, with a profound mix of curiosity and happiness: as if we have been brought here, into his world, to surprise him, to entertain him. He is wholly pleased with our presence.

I've rotated through the Babies' Room, and am standing at the threshold. The toddler—maybe twenty-five yards away— waves at me, smiling hugely, and what else can I do, standing there in that doorway, but smile at him, and wave back?

The next room is filled with adults, all of them lying down on their backs on wooden slatted tables, as were the babies. Most of their mouths are still open in mid-scream. You wouldn't have believed mouths could open that wide. One of the men has his arm raised, his index finger extended; he is pointing upward.

"Maybe he was seeing something," our guide says. "Maybe he was saying God is watching this."

Many of the women still have both hands clasped over their groins. One man clutches his back as if complaining of a backache; only secondarily do you notice that much of his head is missing. Here, as everywhere else, they were begging to be shot. Some of them are covering their faces. Our guide is weeping again, and has to leave the room to compose himself.

Like a hotel cleaning crew, or inspectors—though what we are looking for, I cannot say—we pass from room to room. Our guide has recovered somewhat and is protecting himself, it seems, with the detached language of science as he tells us about the memorial's future plans and needs.

"We are performing studies to discover what micro-organisms are destroying their bodies," he says. "The rate of decomposition is very slow, but it is still occurring. The first organism we have found is a fungus. When you touch a body you can see the spores release. In the second stage of our studies we will find the chemicals that will kill the microorganisms. The third stage will be the extraction of all moisture from the body. Then the bodies will be put in special coffins without air. We did not have the time to do this when we first exhumed them. We continue."

He walks briskly now; the days grow so quickly dark on the equator. We follow him around back and then up a long gradual series of flagstone steps. He is walking with businesslike purpose, past many rooms with their doors closed, while the rest of us are moving very slowly, just this side of reeling. The hour is late, it's closing time, yet there is so much more to see.

Finally we reach the top of the long hill, where a vibrant flycatcher of some sort is swooping and swirling in elegant fluttering script against the sky, pursuing tiny insects that we can't see as they rise from that tall rich grass late in the day's cooling. In the easy way of metaphor, it does not go unconsidered by me that some of these little gnats have been swooping around in the crevices between knee joints and elbows, searching for the faintest molecules of non-lime-dusted nutrition, so that the flycatcher too—also commonly known as a scissortail—is feasting upon, and benefiting from, that most awful crop, that awful harvest; and with its mesmerizing, looping swerves, its acrobatic stalls and spins writing beauty across the sky, it could be argued—by a poet, at least, perhaps—that just as there may always be evil in the world, so too will there be attached at least to the edges of all things, like lace or fringe, the residue of beauty; that there is a beauty in the world that strives to seep through loose-fitting seams and seals, to fill the open spaces like a crack of light limning the bottom of a doorway.

It is certainly not enough to outweigh its opposite in our scale of values—or surely anyone's, or anything's—but still, it's beautiful, and we stop at the top of those steps in the late light and watch, our hearts frantic for these brushes of beauty, as the scissortail, so gracefully fitted to this world, swoops and plunges, casting and weaving. We cling to the sight of it, the one thing all evening that we have wanted to see, the one thing we can stare at and feel our hearts being lifted by, rather than bruised and pressed down.

It's not a fair trade. But the heart hungers for beauty, sometimes is starving for beauty, and we absolutely cannot stop staring at the bird's strange and wondrous flight. We are hypnotized, and—or so it feels—momentarily healed.

Our guide stands farther ahead, looking back and watching us. I might be wrong, but I don't think I am: it seems now that he might be a little impatient with our softness. Not just the slowness of our pace, but now what must surely seem like nothing more than birdwatching. And if he is, why not? Maybe he has seen this kind of thing before. He has probably seen all kinds.

Caught between need and decorum—our tiny, ridiculous fey and faint needs for grace, compared to the larger world's business of pushing forward, pushing on, deeper into the green living—we release from the bird, and walk on.

Higher up—at the very tip-top crest—the grass is greener still, though I wouldn't have believed this to be possible. It's like falling down into a vortex of green, like activating never-used green sensors in the brain. And what our guide is telling us now is likewise unfamiliar. We can hear his words, but there is something about them that is different. They are telling a story we have never heard before.

France sent many soldiers to fight against the Tutsi rebel force, he says. They never apologized for this. He's very angry—he who has been so restrained, so sorrowful, thus far—and it seems to us that for him this last indignity, this last assault, is not seventeen years gone by.

"In 1991 and 1992, France trained the *interahamwe*," he says. "They trained young Hutus." The United States was concerned, but "France convinced the U.S. that France could handle 'the rising tensions.'" He tells us that France did not say anything to the U.S. about the previous killings, between 1975 and 1990, when France, theoretically, was keeping the peace in Rwanda.

France had soldiers stationed at this very site as part of what was called Operation Turquoise—ostensibly to protect refugees—but the French troops, our guide tells us, would "let some Hutu soldiers in to do bad things." He points to a weedsprung road some distance below us and tells us that there was a roadblock there. This was where the French soldiers gave the marauding Hutus entrance into the camp.

"They came as peacekeepers," he tells us, "but they protected the government of killers."

He points to one of the deep pits from which the bodies were exhumed. "French soldiers were playing volleyball there," he says, his voice thick. The bodies were buried, stacked twenty feet deep, and then the road graders leveled the earth over them to make a nice flat volleyball court, one with a view that must have been—again, that word—beautiful.

Where are the old volleyball players now, I wonder? Who won, who lost? Did they play with verve, with spirit?

We walk through another bombed-out, fire-gutted building, another building that, despite the breeze and open air, still retains the familiar scent of blood. Blood in the soil, and, again, blood in the stacks of bundled clothes, saved, preserved, against any possible desire to revise or even erase the testimony of this soil, this place.

We've lingered. We've staggered, strung out all over the

premises, each absorbed in our own heavy little bubble. Back at the visitors' center, one of the custodians is working with hot tar, caulking some seams on the side of the new building. He's got equipment laid out everywhere, and is struggling with a heavy box; I stop to help him lift it, and when we have it repositioned, he wants to shake my hand. I can tell I'm going to get tar on my hand from doing so—he has forgotten, or is unaware—but so what? I'll scrub it off later.

Again, we thank our guide; again, we drop our donation— a hefty five-thousand-franc bill, or about eight U.S. dollars; money that once upon a time could have bartered for death by bullet rather than machete—into the collection box. I go to the restroom to try to rub the tar off my hands—the guide has thoughtfully gone and gotten some kind of petroleum solvent—and with long hard scrubbing, I am finally able to get most, though not all of it, off.

We drive back through Butare, and in the early evening, drop François off at his house. It feels like there's not much to say— like we've said most of it already.

His home is at the end of another long and barely passable road. A high fence surrounds it, and the springtime blossoms in the yard blaze even in the gloom, sending out a deep fragrance; but still, as he smiles and waves good-night to us, and good-bye, he looks old, he looks tired.

We ride away with the windows open and listen to the fantastic night-calls of birds. Our next stop is the small town where Elizabeth has been staying with her relatives; we drop her off at the tiny grocery store, where she has just seen her sister go inside. Our farewells to her feel likewise truncated, incomplete, off-balance; somehow, tomorrow, she must be back at work at Nyamata, while we are largely done with such things. We will be traveling on through the night, far to the north, up toward the national park, where, early in the morning, we are expected to be on the march. It doesn't seem to me that we can get there in a night—that we can pass from what we have seen at Murambi on toward the high-altitude cold of a rainforest, where a few hundred members of a magical other-species wander around the rim of an overgrown, inactive volcano. But that is our goal, that is our intention, and we drive carefully, following the dark road; and now and again, like flares going off in the night, the spoken wishes of the students, their hopes and dreams—their belief in us—ignite in our heads, rising up and illuminating our souls in a way that is not entirely lacking in discomfort. We are still so unfamiliar with all of this. With everything.

Is it American of us to trust that we can get to where we are going without even a map or phone—just the name of some lodge out in the mountains? Or would it have been more American to have worried overmuch, even obsessed, printing up all manner of maps and directions, hiring a driver, etc.? American or not, we are lost. We make our way back up the long dark road to Kigali, where we gas up and ask for directions to Ruhengeri; we know that the lodge is somewhere near there. The attendant tells us we have passed the unmarked turn-off, that we should go back south three kilometers and turn west, cross a bridge, and start up the steep mountain road.

I find the mysterious junction, made more obscure by the fog and darkness, and start up the road with that distinct feeling that an adventure is beginning. I know that the genocide reached Ruhengeri as well—there is no place it did not reach—but for some reason I feel that that portion of our journey is behind us now; there is a part of me that feels more secure now that we are moving up into the mountains. Kigali and Butare were fascinating, but there is simply something good that happens in me when the ground begins to pitch upward, and I'd be silly to try to deny it. To avoid reveling in this leap of the heart—to pay it no attention—would be a terrible waste of life.

But as if the atmosphere of our vehicle must obey some approximation of equilibrium, no sooner do my spirits begin to ascend than do those of certain other passengers dip a bit. How much free will do any of us possess, really? Are our paths truly our own, or are our trails and destinies always governed by an amalgamation of the routes of so many others, as one thread or braid of river is always but a spinning part of the rest?

"They said this road would be well paved," says one passenger. Already, our pavement has vanished; the road—though wide—has gone to dirt. There is no other traffic. But where else can the road lead? We have already gained significant elevation; the lights of Kigali, glimpsed only as brief necklaces of light through the heavy roadside foliage, lie far below.

"There's barely any road at all," says another passenger. "This is the *worst* road."

I would stop and ask for directions—I truly would!—but there is no one, only dark forest and fog and steeply winding switchbacks. And to find mountain gorillas, we need to go into the mountains, right?

To suspect one has taken a wrong turn, and to be pushing ahead anyway, up a rutted, winding road, in a foreign country, and so late at night: I understand the fretfulness. But I'm confident these are the precise directions the gas-station attendant gave us—and also that there is only one road from Kigali to Ruhengeri, up and over the mountains.

"Maybe the road's being upgraded," I say. "Maybe they've torn up all the old asphalt and are paving it with something new." I stop and get out and try to find evidence for this hypothesis, but can't.

"Maybe after they tear up the old asphalt, they load it into trucks and carry it away," I say.

The other passengers want me to turn around and go back and ask the gas-station attendant for directions again. Or ask someone else, back down in Kigali. But Kigali is far below and beyond us now. It seems to me that the best way to find out if this is the right road is to go on farther.

The night feels so *good*. Wherever we are, it's clearly in the middle of nowhere, and the fog is so dense now that I finally find a place to stop. We get out and I stand there again in the blackness, unable to see even my hand in front of my face. I find myself overwhelmed by a delicious combination of relief—actual or physical distance from the heaviness of all that we've heard and seen—and the joy of being up on the mountain, in the forest.

"Let's go a little farther on," I say. "I just can't picture this being a road to nowhere."

What do I know about Rwanda? Nothing.

After another ten minutes—which to my fellow passengers feel I'm sure like an hour—we pass one lone bar-looking kind of place, a dim light back in the woods. No one suggests we stop. Sometimes you just don't have a good feeling.

Discomfort, if not yet full-fledged fear, continues to thicken within our car. I crack the window a tiny bit, as if to let some of the tension out. In my luggage I've brought a hunting knife, and in the darkness I stop to retrieve it, unbeknownst to the other passengers; they assume I am looking for a flashlight.

We'll go just a little bit farther.

The dirt road is becoming more muddy, higher up; the fog is such that we need our windshield wipers. We pass another bar, this one a little larger; but fog-shrouded as it is, it just doesn't look that inviting. We don't know where we're headed, I realize—only now do I realize this, really—but I still think this has to be the right road. I will confess, however, that the subtle but steady concern emanating from my companions now begins to eat away at my hopes.

And then, as if my own dimming spirits have conjured difficulty, the road becomes soupy with rutted puddles, and suddenly we find ourselves faced with a profound obstacle—an abandoned military vehicle, one of those giant semi-amphibious tank-treaded things: a wraith in the fog, unoccupied.

Two thoughts torch my mind simultaneously. (How quickly the mind flashes and burns, when it is fed the fuel of adrenaline!) The way the truck is positioned to face us, square in the center of the road, makes it look like an archetypal ambush set-up—the kind that outlaws have been preparing since time immemorial. I immediately check the rear-view to be sure that our backtrail has not been cut off.

The other thought, though less alarming, is not all cheery either—the big truck may simply be stuck. And if an all-terrain, go-anywhere transport vehicle has been defeated by this road, then what business have we attempting it ourselves?

There is barely room to pass. There *might* be room to pass, though it's possible that this is a sure way to get stuck. My heart's hammering. Why don't we turn back? Why don't we drive back down to Kigali, get a room, and abandon our hopes of seeing gorillas in the morning?

Instead, slowly, we ease our way around, deeper into the fog.

On the far side of the army truck, the dirt road tapers, narrows to less than two lanes. What gall, or hope, had I possessed to think that the thread of my desire alone would be sufficient to lead us to one small lodge in a country for which we have no map at all?

There are no billboards, no street signs; we don't even know the language. We've traveled maybe half a mile farther when I finally admit defeat.

Newly American, ever-American, we grasp at our technology. Terry has an old clunker cell phone, which doesn't receive calls in Rwanda but which, amazingly, can dial out. She calls Louis, her adopted son, who's back in Salt Lake, where it is not nearing midnight but is instead the broad middle of the day. We're hoping he might somehow be able to describe for us where we are going and how to get there, to sort it out on his computer, but it's no use—we can't figure out how to tell him where we are. We started out heading west from Kigali, of course, but we could be anywhere now.

Still, it's good to hear his calm voice there in the darkness: a point of connection in the fog. He sides with my passengers,

and warns us against pushing on farther, lost at this hour; turn
back to Kigali, he says, and get a room for the night. The real
road to Ruhengeri is a good one, he says, well-paved. Not a
dirt road.

I can hear the relief in the voices of my companions as we
discuss this reasonable advice. The problem is that our permit
for gorilla-viewing, gotten months in advance, is for seven
in the morning. It's not the end of the world if we don't see
gorillas, but I'm just not quite ready to give up.

Still, it's definitely time to turn around. We do so, back-
tracking around the mysteriously stalled military vehicle—
passing it with all the tension with which a mule might
sidestep a rattlesnake—and head back toward Kigali, at least
an hour back down the mountain. Maybe we can get better
directions. I'll drive through the night if I have to. I might as
well admit that I really want to see the gorillas.

After a while, we reach the first lone cinderblock bar, the
one that looked so unappealing to us previously. It looks no less
so, this much later, and we pass by again, going in the opposite
direction, but when I do the math—hours more of driving,
versus stopping and going inside for two minutes to ask for
directions—it suddenly looks less daunting. I turn around yet
again, and park. Terry and I get out and walk toward the dimly
lit bar, pale specters in the fog.

The bar is filled with people. We pause and peer inside,
nod *maraho* to the men who are in the doorway and spilling out
into the parking area—beyond them, it's standing room only.
Inside, the atmosphere is charged with tension, expectation,
anticipation, and my first thought is that perhaps it's a late-
night Gacaca court—a backwoods tribunal. I've just about

opened my mouth to speak when everyone in the bar explodes with near-deafening exclamations, howls, roars; and as if I have crossed some electric threshold, one which has directly caused the eruption, I step back quickly, thinking, I should have driven back to Kigali.

It's just a soccer game, is all. Maybe some regional tournament, I don't know—I'm not a big soccer fan. Whoever has just scored, they are sure happy about it, and a more auspicious omen to accompany our arrival could not have been imagined. The men around us are leaping up and down, thrusting their arms skyward in the same manner with which the professor received Cairo's poem, and in between that initial wave of celebration and the next, we take the opportunity to ask—after first inquiring who just scored, as if it is a matter of primary importance to us as well—where the road to Ruhengeri is.

The young man we've decided to address does not speak English, but he understands our question—Ruhengeri?—and the expression on his face is unmistakable. But of course, it is that way. He gestures in the direction from which we have just come. Back up the dirt road, past the defunct truck.

We thank him, wish him and his team well, and go back to our car, proceeding now with our confidence restored. It's a big difference.

Ruhengeri is quiet when we roll in, as it should be, given that it's after midnight. The wide streets are empty; even the bars have emptied. Perhaps thanks to its proximity to the national park, there are several touristy-looking curio shops, hotels, and theme bars, the most alarming of which (to our eyes) is Club Texas, or something like that. We drive slowly, looking for an establishment that calls itself Gorilla's Nest.

We don't see it—there's a Sky Gorilla Lodge, but it's closed—and we decide to take the road out of town that goes up toward the national park, said to be only thirteen kilometers distant. (There's also a sign that tells us we're nearing the Ugandan border, which, though we have no reason to be concerned, somehow makes us uneasy: as if it is any different to be lost and adrift in Uganda rather than Rwanda. What a curious, swirling, irrational construct the mind is!)

We wander various roads, finding no lodges. When we come to an open gate, we lose our nerve again—what right do we have to be here? What if this is a back road into another country?—and turn back down the mountain to Ruhengeri. There we finally spy another human—a man filling up his battered, wired-together little motorcycle at a gas station. I stop and ask for directions.

He and the attendant don't speak much English either. I write the name of our lodge down on a sheet of paper, *Gorilla's Nest*—again, certain expressions are unmistakable, no language is necessary for an accurate interpretation of the letters—and there is at first instantaneous recognition. My heart leaps.

Immediately, though, I realize that he is thinking of another place with the word *Gorilla* in it. He and the attendant point to the word *Nest* and frown.

A solid ten minutes of heated Kinyarwanda ensues— theories, hypotheses, guesses and conjectures, and the degree of disagreement between the two men is not encouraging. But finally, with brio, the motorcycle man fastens his oversized helmet and gestures for us to follow him.

I see now that he is more bedraggled than I had first realized. He's wearing an immense down coat (it is not that cold), which is leaking feathers everywhere, and his eyes are deeply bloodshot; he is—there is no way to sugarcoat this—deeply stoned. But we are so close. We want to see the gorillas.

We follow him back down the road—he's driving very slowly, though I can't help but wonder if in his sleepy mind the road, and the world, is hurtling past at a speed that is barely navigable—and after a short distance he pulls up into the secluded driveway of an opulent hotel that is girded with high, heavy iron bars. He rides his motorcycle right up to the gate and, without dismounting, jabs insistently at a buzzer.

A well-dressed concierge comes out and peers cautiously through the bars, and it seems to me that much the same conversation ensues. Eventually my little scrap of paper is shoved through, and examined carefully; then the gates swing open. Never could we afford to stay at this place; it's not even worth considering. We are only hoping, it seems, for new directions. Our gorilla trek leaves at dawn. It is now 2 a.m.; we must be up at 5. The hours are melting fast now.

The concierge's demeanor is professional, but every sentence he utters releases a plume of rum vapor so dense it seems you should be able to see it. He is an interesting counterpart to our stoned motorcyclist. His breath spreads and meanders like a wide, sprawling river flowing through the night; it's so powerful that it seems like the snap of a cigarette lighter could immolate us all.

But we have nowhere else to turn. After the requisite ten

minutes of exasperated disagreements, the concierge tells us to follow the man who's led us here: he will take us up the mountain, we are told, if we pay him for his time.

We do so happily. I've already given him some gas money, but now that we've been offered his services for hire, it feels somehow more professional—in narrow American thinking, more like we can now expect him to provide the hoped-for outcome. We thank the concierge and take off into the night, following the wandering, weaving, lone red taillight of our guide as he putters through a neighborhood and then, once out of town, through forests and fields, with only their edges illuminated by our headlights.

The fog returns. We're so tired, and the lone red light is becoming hypnotic, as is the snail's pace of our progress; at one point another motorcycle comes up from behind us and passes us at a corner before proceeding on into the night.

What a ragged advance we are making! Once again, concern and doubt begin to appear among our passengers; fatigue, darkness, and the absence of any map whatsoever begin to rewire the circuits of confidence in our minds. We start to question whether we are even still following the right motorcycle—we all four swear to each other that now it seems certain that there are two people on the one in front of us. We're *pretty* certain we saw the one motorcycle pass our leader's. But maybe we glanced away. Maybe it only passed us. Or maybe ours passed the second one, during a turn, after it had just been passed itself. Maybe we are lost again.

The road narrows and becomes more winding. The motorcycle in front of us is speeding up and then slowing down; it appears that the person driving it has no head. We know this is not possible—in no way are we fooled—but it does not make us happy to be following even the visual representation of a headless horseman. It's easy, looking back, to call us silly, but I have to tell you, there somewhere near the Congo around two in the morning, it's just plain spooky. We proceed on faith.

In time we come to a tiny crossroads. Our guide stops at a bar where the other motorcycle is waiting; we see that the second man is alone and in possession of a head, and that our guide, too, is toting no other passenger, nor is he headless. The wind had simply been ballooning his giant coat. While we wait, he visits awhile with his fellow motorcyclist—again, at length—and then, like desperadoes, having apparently chosen to fall in together, they jet off up the road, choosing what is far and away the less-traveled path, ignoring the sign that points out that the national park is to the right.

We follow them a long way. They are riding side-by-side, conversing as they go. We pass a sign that says UGANDA BORDER CROSSING AHEAD, and my passengers—who, it will be remembered, are all women—inform me in no uncertain terms that their instincts and intuitions have just crossed over from uncomfortable into full-on freak-out.

I understand what they're saying. I'm uncomfortable too. But it seems to me if they were going to attack us, they would have attempted it. And I don't really fear the stoned motorcyclist, though his mysterious compatriot is a bit of a wild card. Nor do I want to appear to be the distrustful American, afraid of our dark-skinned Samaritans.

But the most important thing, I know, is to teach Lowry to trust her instincts. It's important to let Elizabeth and Terry make the call, no matter what my own read is on the situation. Turn back, they tell me, and although I'm convinced they are wrong, I know that they are also right. I make a big U-turn in the muddy road and begin directing us to the national park.

I'm surprised by how upset this makes our guide. Having noticed our retreat, he wheels around and races after us, pulls up alongside, and shouts, yells, gestures as best he can—as if to say, *So close, only a little farther; so close!*

His yelling does nothing to calm the concerns of my companions, and for the first time I feel a little uncertainty myself. I don't see how this strange and slightly addled man can possibly manufacture a plan to overcome us, but what do I know? He's upset; I tell myself it's because he really wants to help us. Boy is he hot, though: yelling with true anger. That's just the marijuana talking, I tell myself. We have not harmed him.

We proceed blithely up toward the formal park entrance, where we finally encounter a lodge: Gorilla Mountain, I think was the name of it, not Gorilla's Nest. I get out and knock on all the doors, hoping to find someone who can give me directions, but it's darker than the inside of a cow; nobody answers, and no lights come on. Our motorcycle friend, meanwhile, walks with me like an unseen shadow, darkness within darkness, and sometimes tugs impatiently at my jacket, his eyes fiercely bloodshot in the beam of my little penlight, his big coat reeking of pot. He fumbles with his cell phone, trying, I think, to call the concierge at the opulent hotel back down in Ruhengeri, but there's no coverage, and he curses vehemently.

I want to apologize to him, but I don't regret my choice. It is more important to be wrong, and rude to a stranger, than to try to browbeat the instincts of family and friends. I have done so once already, in refusing to turn back to Kigali; so what if I'm right this time, too?

Our guide, oblivious to all of this, keeps gesturing back toward the direction we came from—toward the other road. I go back to our car and tell my passengers that I think we should go that way again—that we've tried our best, on this path, and that he seems pretty convinced. I tell them that he's kind of a gentle fellow, and that I'm not worried about physical harm. We're all relieved that the other motorcycle has gone on—doubtless exasperated with the crazy, wandering Americans—and in light of that development, we reach a consensus decision: that it will be all right to go back down the first road so long as the second motorcycle doesn't show up.

Imagine please the tiny complexity of feelings I experience when our long-suffering guide, with his blatting little engine skipping and straining, pulls slowly into a shaded copse beside which there is a very small and absolutely unilluminated sign identifying our destination: GORILLA'S NEST. Relief, even jubilation, shame, certainly, guilt, and yet, no regret—none. The world can be a hard place, and when the heart in the night, informed by nothing more than one's deepest instincts, says to *go*, it is time to go; the integrity of that dim spark, that human fire, must be honored.

The world can be a beautiful place, too. Looking around, we realize that we have arrived in Paradise. The parking area is surrounded by all sorts of night-blooming blossoms, many of them ghostly white in the dark, and the fragrance is overwhelming. Because the rooms were not expensive by American standards, we had expected a bungalow; an online search revealed that previous guests had complained about the cold night air, and the lack of electricity after dark. But those people must have been crazy. The spacious lodge is lit tastefully, back in the forest, and at nearly three a.m. it seems like a dream.

I thank our guide, press another five thousand francs on him—eight more dollars, though of course no price can absolve our debt to him; I simply have to decide on my own whether to carry that weight any further forward—and rather than bolting as I had hoped and expected him to do, he insists on helping us with our bags and making sure the lodge staff knows that we have arrived.

And then, as if in a dream, elegantly dressed men in white suits appear from the farthest recesses of the elegant lobby, back in the forest. The wood floors and check-in counter are hewn from some species we have never seen before and which is probably no longer legal to cut; the high vaulted roof overhead is an intricately woven coil of tight fiber, like that of a great basket. And here at the bottom of it we find ourselves, the only guests, being tended, our solicitors having waited for us all this time, simply watching and waiting, and keeping things in lovely, perfect order for all the long hours and perhaps days preceding.

Our guide, having seen us into their hands, zips up his heavy coat and departs. We spend the ensuing moments staring agape at the splendor, feeling almost crushed by the attentiveness and concern, the accumulated worry on our behalf—worry, hope, and yet faith on the part of the staff that we would finally make our way to the place that they have made ready. I find the solicitousness of the manager particularly touching. He's proud of the beauty he's been tasked with maintaining. He doesn't own the lodge, he explains, but he's expected to keep it beautiful. We do our best to tell him that he has.

We are not allowed to carry any of our bags; three attendants shoulder everything, and lead us, with the pencil-thin wavering blue light of their headlamps, out of the lodge and through another, even more spectacular garden in the back. I am reminded, as we make our way, that just as the night is capable of eliciting from us or in us a response of deep fear, so too is it able to ignite a deep awareness, a greater awareness, of a beauty that we might overlook in the daytime. What a tangled thicket our minds are, and how we labor, often with great futility, to shove or force individual thin strands of desire, like faintly illuminated beams, through that dark and mysterious bramble: pushing, pushing, pushing. Surely there are times to push—our minds are to some extent our own, and we are responsible for their care and upkeep—but surely too there are older, far more established paths and avenues—more graceful routes—to be discovered or encountered, now and again, by not always thrashing around in that thicket of fear and beauty? Surely someone, somewhere else—some Other—has plenty of light, and is far wiser at directing those thin beams of ours through the vast dark.

I'm giddy with exhaustion. We follow our new guides through the back garden, where a fountain is gurgling, and beneath a magical canopy of giant eucalyptus trees, seeming in the perspective of night to be as tall as the stars. The flagstone walkway wends its way around numerous garden cottages; in the darkness we can only see their silhouettes.

There are no other guests—all of paradise is ours, and there are so many rooms to choose from.

As if the evening could become any more surreal, we follow the trace of thin blue light across what turns out to be a narrow wooden suspension bridge. We cross a little creek, a ravine, and pass through a dense patch of rainforest where sound becomes muted and the air still. Then we are out the other side, and crossing a wide, well-kept lawn, bound for the farthest rooms, and with that final bridge-crossing it feels that only now are the skulls far enough behind us that we can fully set them down. As if, though there is no cure or antidote for terror and evil, the massive application of beauty can nonetheless in certain instances bring a stillness to the torments of guilt and doubt, or even to the scars of the wounds themselves. I cannot speak to the latter idea, of course; clearly, we are not the wounded. We are merely the guilty and the confused. But still, so great is the balm of the garden's beauty upon us that it seems possible to believe in the miraculous benefits of such beauty, even while knowing how improbable it is that the bulk of those so deeply afflicted by the evil of the past would have any hope whatsoever of passing over that rainslicked footbridge, one hand gripping the heavy suspension cables for balance. This place, we are all too aware, has been built for us, not them. Are we somehow extracting, exploiting, colonizing?

But to have feared, only an hour or two ago, that we might be machine-gunned, no matter how absurd those fears—no matter how distant from reality—and then within that same span of an hour or two, after having been lost, to be found, and to be lying down on clean sheets in a warm room with renewed hopes of seeing gorillas in only a few more hours: what would it be like to live every day within the exuberant amplitudes of such wild possibility? What garden is this into which we've been released? It would be exhausting, I'm sure, frazzle-inducing; and yet, here in the midst of it, it is so alluring. Could one consciously step off the usual paths of routine—as if stepping purposefully, and with nothing more than faith or instinct, from a well-illuminated life to the edge of darkness—and find this slightly different, and perhaps slightly fuller or more intriguing existence, at will? Or is it the very rarity of such experiences—such strange days and nights—that gives them their value?

I do not understand how this can be shared. I do not understand how 11 million Rwandans—nor even the ghosts of one million—can make it across that bridge. And more than anything—the most vexing question of all—I do not understand why we have been allowed to cross it ourselves.

We sleep without dreams, Terry and Low in one garden cottage and Elizabeth and I in the next. We sleep the slumber known to the traveler who has pressed on beyond the territory of exhaustion; we rest, as if hibernating, in that state of limbo for two hours, until we are awakened by a light knocking on the glass door and the faintest light of equatorial pre-dawn.

On our feet again, we walk quietly through the vast garden, back across the swag-bellied footbridge, the ancient hardwood planks gleaming, and along the circuitous flagstone walkway to the cavernous restaurant, in which we are the only diners. We are attended to by a waitstaff of four; back in the gleaming kitchen, half a dozen chefs in gleaming white uniforms squeeze fresh fruit for our juice, mangos and papayas, and prepare omelets over low blue flames. This is not who

I am, and I don't understand how I got here. I do not want to spend all my days observing and cataloguing blade-sliced skulls, but nor do I want to stay here in paradise forever. What do I want? It occurs to me that I don't know—that perhaps I have not been thinking enough about the level of life I wish to occupy. Not too deep—not subterranean—not all the time, but not too shallow. Where?

More than ever, here in Rwanda, I suspect that we may all be nothing more than an absurd accident occurring far out on the tree of life. I know that risks sounding like blasphemy— that the improbability of our existence, and our survival, and even more so these inexplicable moments of extreme bounty, can just as surely give strong credence to the idea or belief or even the faith that we are special, that we have been chosen, and that there is a plan to integrate us into an already-made and waiting world. But whenever I look back over my shoulder, I see as much evidence—an equal balance of evidence—that could point to absolute randomness. What other mechanism or guidance could account for all this?

One of the lodge's managers, Felix, drives us to the park. We're late; we've taken more time, after our feast, to gather all our many things—gaiters, raingear, cold-weather jackets and fleece, hats, gloves, video cameras, still cameras, notebooks, water bottles—and then there's the matter of displaced or misplaced paperwork, the permits we purchased and brought with us. I think briefly of the status cards that all Rwandans were once required to carry with them always, which identified them as Hutu, Tutsi, or Twa, and which determined the fate, the destiny, of so many—of how if the paper identification, much-creased over a lifetime of being folded and unfolded, was lost, or ruined by water, or simply wore away, someone's life could be changed forever. But it's an unpleasant thought, an uncomfortable one, and so I simply file it far away, out of the inconvenient sight of my consciousness. What is the responsibility of a charmed life?

Up in the park, there are other groupings of fellow tourists, other nationalities—from Germany, Italy, France, Spain— and, valid permit-holders that they are, on-time arrivees and standers-in-line who seem to have understood intuitively what is required, they are already lining up with their guides, visiting and preparing to depart.

After some fluttering of passports and the intervention on our behalf of Felix—the visage of the park official seems to express absolutely the dreaded and universal response, *I'm sorry, we don't appear to have any reservations for Williams or Bass*—a last-minute guide is procured for us, one who I suspect had been scheduled for an off-day. Frances Ndagijimana gathers us off to the side, away from the other, larger groups—we will have him, and each other, to ourselves—and gives us the short preparatory course on mountain gorillas required of all visitors. He explains the nature of the agreement between Rwanda, Uganda, and the Congo, where all share equitably in the income generated from gorilla tourism; this income is helping to protect and save the gorillas, he tells us, so we should feel very good about coming this far to see them.

Because they are so accustomed to being viewed, we're told, the animals will allow us to approach pretty much as close as want—but it's imperative, Frances says, that we not draw any closer than ten meters, and that we not cough or sneeze in their direction. They share 99 percent of our genes, he reminds us, but because they live in isolation on the tops and flanks of old extinct volcanoes, their immune systems have in no way been exposed to the wild variances and mutations of viruses that daily inhabit us, in ever-shifting fashion—nor, Frances points out, have we necessarily been exposed to theirs. But the concern here is the gorillas. This is their last redoubt. Where once they roamed freely through these three nations, numbering perhaps as many as a hundred thousand, according to biologist George Schaller, there are now less than eight hundred left in the wild—480 ranging back and forth across the border between Rwanda and the Congo, and another 300 in Uganda.

There is so much that is curious about them. Europeans did not lay eyes on these creatures—did not name and describe them for the scientific community, had not even imagined this dark furry version or jungle-reflection of the self—until 1903. Schaller presciently fretted that they might become the first major vertebrate to be discovered and go extinct in the same century.

They have been killed for food by starving villagers, and killed for sport by murderous white men with twisted, boiling psyches. Entire families—parents, aunts, uncles, siblings, grandparents—have been slaughtered so that a single newborn could then be extracted for the benefit of an acquisitive zoo in some distant country; and the newborns, far more often than not, have failed to survive the journey, or if surviving that then not the arrival, not the new country, not the new life: not the eternal estrangement, for the sake of our oblivious, adoring eyes, from the loving arms of a close and extended family.

This park was created in 1925, soon after Belgium took control of Rwanda. It's where the charismatic and controversial Dian Fossey lived, studied, and worked before being killed in 1985. Since that time, 160 guards have been murdered in the park; they must seek to protect the gorillas not only from poachers but from revenge-killings by rebels in one country or another who seek to weaken the government of either their own nation or a neighboring one. They must contend with tree poachers, too, who covet the biggest trees in the park for their slash-and-burn potential as charcoal, that seductive industry.

It's a small park; the gorillas are packed in pretty tight. There might be more vegetative diversity and biomass in this lush equatorial garden than almost anywhere else on earth, but it is still, so far as wildlife goes, a very small and contained garden. This is the place where they come from, the place where they were first made—arising here as if in direct relationship with the volcanoes that once blossomed in this garden likewise—and it is here, at the point of their beginning, where they will be making their last stand. The world seems so large and daunting and complicated, and the garden so small, that it is hard to imagine any number of visitors, each of them throwing a few hundred dollars at the problem, that would be sufficient to stave off the end result of extinction, that final vanishing. In the meantime, there are 780 of these creatures left.

It's such a small garden that a low rock wall surrounds it; the land protected, in theory. It's as if the park is one single cell, I think, with a semipermeable membrane, a distinct and finite membrane; and a governance and economy, a whir of miracles, going on within. Are some cells more valuable and important to the body than others? Surely so. And surely, this last garden of gorillas is important to Rwanda, to Africa, to the world: more so than we can or will probably ever know. But there are so many outside factors—the great fiery gearworks of the world's gestures and respirations, proceeding sometimes in concert with the little whirrings of that cell and sometimes without regard for it.

In our mini-tutorial, Frances tells us that there are eighteen groups of gorillas in the park—some accessible to tourists, and others protected from them. (I'm thinking of the story Terry told me about some rich-ass corporate type who, when he first saw a silverback, jumped to his feet and began beating his silly middle-aged chest.) The subadults, Frances goes on, are between six and eight years old, and are called blackbacks. The older males begin to develop silver hair in the small of their backs—the distinctive saddle—around their twelfth year. A female does not conceive until her eighth year; she will spend three and a half years weaning her offspring, usually one child but sometimes two. A gorilla typically lives thirty-five to forty-five years; a mother will bear four to six babies in a lifetime. They hardly ever drink water, receiving all their moisture instead from the lush vegetation they feed upon— nearly seventy pounds' worth each day. A big silverback can weigh nearly five hundred pounds. They do not swim, are loath to wade across a creek or river of even ankle-deep water, and will instead seek a fallen log to use as a bridge. They sleep all night, each in a nest of his or her own making, on a pallet of soft vegetation. Each morning, Frances tells us, "The chief beats on his chest to wake them up."

"I can see that you are very excited," he says—speaking not just to Lowry, but all of us. He asks us how far we would like to walk to see gorillas. There is a group that we can reach in only an hour; or, if we wish, we can walk a very long way, through inclement weather and terrain. Many visitors, surprisingly, choose the latter course, curious to go as far up the mountain as possible—to see the cabin that was Dian Fossey's research station, and the site where she was killed.

Our group decides on the short walk—the hour's journey. There's a bit of a drive involved, but from there, we should have a fairly leisurely ascent: up through farmers' fields, across the low stone dividing wall, and into the rainforest.

The group we will seek out, Frances tells us, is called the Kwitonda group. "It means 'to be humble,'" he says. My heart starts beating faster. Is it really going to happen?

The Kwitonda group belongs to both the Congo and Rwanda, Frances explains; they range back and forth across the border. He reassures us that there will be no trouble—that the guards in both countries are committed to protecting and sharing the gorillas. They first came over into Rwanda, apparently, to escape the fighting in the Congo. Refugees, even in their own last refuge. As for Rwanda's own antagonists, Frances says, "We walk together. On this issue, we are brothers and sisters."

I don't ask him which he is—which ethnicity. Forgive me, but I'm tired of it. We've crossed over that bridge, the one with the night-blooming trumpet lilies, and we're supposed to be in paradise. It's possible that we are.

We get back in our private vehicle and drive slowly through the countryside, past bare open fields of rich black earth in which women with hoes scratch, scratch, scratch. Children run barefooted down the road alongside us, shrieking with joy. Do we really inhabit the same world, or are there different levels, other levels we catch glimpses of, now and again, as if seeing such things through brief openings in the clouds?

Frances has studied hard to become a guide. For the thirty-seven trainee slots available when he applied, there were two thousand applicants from around the country. It's not quite like passing through the eye of a needle, but it's pretty close. I'm fascinated by the relationship the gorillas have with the volcanoes, and ask him about it; "If there is any danger, the animals smell it," he says, speaking of the magma just beneath the surface. "The cows, the goats—everything leaves. They know."

Cut down the tall trees, I think. *Cut down the tall trees tonight.*

Six of the volcanoes are inactive, jungle-swarmed, birth-givers to the rainforest that shrouds them now, and to these rich fields below; two are active, still bleeding fire, still being born. There's a part of me that wants to imagine the gorillas living right at the edge of that fire, passing through the wilting vegetation and luxuriating in the vapors, while marveling, in the night, at the hissing red-eyed dollops and gurgles of lava—lulled to sleep, perhaps, by the earth's intestinal rumbles and shifts, and knowing that here, at the edge of ruin (as well as the edge of perpetual rebirth), they might be safest of all. But Frances says no, no, the gorillas are at least as cautious with volcanoes and fire as they are with rivers and creeks. They, like all animals, avoid the places where the earth trembles and threatens to erupt; they prefer the safe places.

The babies can be born at any time of year, just as with

humans. The newborns are given their names by the guides each June; sometimes they are named for the site of their birth. Kabafwa, a hill in the park; Gihishamwotsi, another hill. Of late, many of the young gorillas have been dying.

"We don't know why they don't survive," Frances says.

The road becomes less than a road, rockier and more rutted than anything we have seen yet. There are still people everywhere, but only along the path: above us and around us, there are mountains, still forested, with a quiltwork of small farms—potato fields, mostly—creeping up the flanks steadily, like flames clearing the skirt of the forest. I don't know what they would plant if the blight came through the way it did in Europe. I don't know. I'm a good worrier.

Everywhere, children are carrying bundles of branches on their heads. People of my lower-middle-class economic strata tend to lament, here in the new normal of the Great Recession (and yet here I am in Africa, having gotten an assignment, flown here on miles), how our days have become so uncertain, our incomes and expenditures taking on a fiendish hand-to-mouth, hunter-gatherer quality; this, however, is the real thing. And these sojourners have to travel farther up the mountain each day to scavenge enough branches to have so much as a cook-fire.

Every girl we see over the age of about eight carries a baby on her back, towel-swaddled. None of them appear beaten or defeated; each seems engaged with the day, and interested in our passage. At one point Terry stops and gets out and takes some Polaroid pictures, then distributes them to the children. Magic from far away: it can happen on any day.

Frances's walkie-talkie beeps and crackles; he answers

it, has a brief conversation in Kinyarwanda, then hangs up, animated. "They say the gorillas are out in the fields this morning," he says. "It's very rare. Maybe they will still be out there. We can hurry now."

And we do, slithering up the mud road, past the final stick-hut and adobe dwellings, and out into one of the vast patchwork hillside fields where boys and women are scattered, working, rotator cuffs and lumbar muscles and deltoids doing the silent labor of tractors. Fantastic lenses of fog and rainclouds drift through the rift valley far below us, as if scouring the earth in the same fashion in which glaciers once carved out the valleys around my home in Montana, but we're above those rainclouds; up here, it's sunny and almost warm. Not quite—we'll start out wearing our fleece—but the mild sun as well as the slope of the mountain, and the wet, rich, heavy bare soil underfoot, will soon have us peeling down to a single layer.

Many of the children in the fields are shirtless, and the women, certainly, wear no jackets, no layers, only their brightly colored blouses tucked inside their long *kangas* wrapped tight.

A tiny cluster of young men meet us when we stop at the mud-road's end; two of them, trailcutters, will assist Frances in the guiding. There are some shirts and walking sticks for sale; Terry buys one of the latter, and we promise Lowry one of the former upon our return. Something with a gorilla on it, a souvenir to wear to school. It's hard to imagine going back home, being back in school. We thought long and hard about taking her out of school for ten days, here in the second half of her sophomore year; her test scores and grades will now, we worry, sag a bit—her counselor warned us of as much—but we all decided this was the opportunity of a lifetime. Every day I'm a little bothered by the fear that our choice was an irresponsible one, and that worse, it teaches such by example; but here we are, leaning up the trail toward the forest and the park, which is now only about a mile away. Somewhere back in the United States her geometry teacher is drawing complicated proofs and theorems on the blackboard. Is it peculiarly American to want everything, everything, and particularly for your children, or is that a universal desire?

The soil is so rich. Baby potatoes spill from the ground, are dislodged by our footsteps—we are disrupting a tilled and cultivated field—and we try to avoid them where we can. The gorillas have gone back into the rainforest, Frances says. The little white potatoes gleam like tiny skulls. Clouds find us, spit and then spray rain—we stop and pull on our rainjackets— and then the sun comes back out. It's like walking uphill in a sauna, and it feels great to be on the move, with no idea whatsoever of the specifics of what we will be seeing, only that we hope to find the gorillas at some point in the day. They have not been promised to us, but we have faith.

When we find them, or if we do, we will have exactly, precisely, one hour with them. It's a number the guides and researchers have settled on, one which satisfies the visitors yet does not stress or strain the animals too much.

The soil is so incredibly black, so incredibly rich and slick and muddy. The walking sticks were not a scam; they would have been a good idea for all of us. From time to time Frances stops and shows us some one certain plant that the gorillas like to eat: gooseberry, or white celery, their favorite. One of the trailcutters, Jerome, uses his machete to cut and peel one of the celery stalks, giving us each a bite to try. It's good, tangier than our domestic celery, with more of a watercress taste—different from "regular" celery in the way that arugula or dandelion leaf is different from spinach or Romaine.

There is so much to marvel at here. The wide valley below, ringed by dark, blue-black mountains; the newly turned fields working their way up the slopes; the villagers out in the fields, working with their hoes, backs bent in ridiculously limber positions—occasionally they straighten up and watch us from a distance as we pass, standing up to gaze at us as if they are merely resting. And the forest, the wall of it, just ahead.

Here and there, in the fields, there stands an occasional eucalyptus tree, seemingly there for no other purpose than to cast a patch of shade, though it is hard at this elevation and in this damp to imagine that this country ever knows real heat, heat greater than the internal warmth generated by one's own labors. Many of the young trees have long scars on them, similar to the markings that deer and elk make on saplings back in Montana, when they are rubbing the summer velvet from their antlers; Frances tells us these have been left by the gorillas, who come out of the park sometimes to peel the bark from the eucalyptus trees and lick the sap. It seems like a hard place to be a eucalyptus tree, with the big ones cut for lumber or charcoal and the young ones being coveted by roving bands of giant primates.

We come to the low rock wall that forms the park boundary: the line between protected land and unprotected, between wild and domestic, jungle and agriculture, darkness and light. It's built of bright red volcanic boulders, the stones riddled with vesicles caused by escaping gases, remnants from back when the clastic material was first hurled into the sky. Frances gives us one last briefing, telling us to make no sound at all, to not sneeze or cough in the gorillas' direction, to leave our bright jackets behind—as if the animals might become contaminated or afflicted by the very sight of us—and above all, to keep our distance. If one of the creatures starts to come our way, he says, we must move back. Sometimes they want to play—especially when they have been feeding on the new bamboo shoots, which can ferment in their stomachs to create alcohol—but even playing, they can easily break a tourist's arm. I want to ask him if this has ever happened—how he knows it to be so—but he already has his finger to his lips, shushing us, and we are moving.

We cross over the wall and into the jungle. The agrarian world, the troubled world, is sealed off behind us. We are in a better place.

There is vegetation everywhere. It's like a child's dream of a jungle, translucent light-pierced fronds dripping from last night's rain and casting a soothing subaqueous light on us. I wouldn't have thought it possible for the humidity to increase, but somehow it has; the broad leaves of the canopies trap nearly every molecule of moisture, every exhalation, every breath: it's warm, here in this magical living realm, and while it is an utterly different world from any I have yet seen, the way forward feels slightly familiar, and slightly comforting.

The guides are moving quickly, following the fresh trail left from the gorillas' morning feeding—it's a swath about the width of a lawn mower, with their humanlike footprints visible wherever the black earth can be glimpsed beneath the lush forbs—and suddenly, ahead of us, our leaders go electric with discovery. Frances whispers that the elephants have been in here this morning—that the trackers have found where the gorillas encountered the elephants, and the two groups moved away from each other. We have just missed much, it seems, but we are about to see much, too.

It's wonderful, how natural and easy our movement is here, all of us striding through the jungle quickly, following in the slipstream of the gorillas' wake, as if such motion is the one that best fits our bodies—the sweep of rotator cuffs, the swell of calf for balance on the soft earth, the slightly forward cant of the body leaning into the jungle, ducking beneath fronds and passing beneath branches. The path the gorillas are making, the path they are choosing, passing between this one tree and another, perambulating along this one contour rather than another, makes ancient and comfortable sense, as does the green dappled light that is shuttering into our brains and filling us with pleasure, with joy. If we had time to stop and evaluate it, it might dissipate; instead, we keep moving forward, following the precise steps of where our gorillas have been.

We smell them before we see them. It is a hard scent to describe, but it is profound; to me, a longtime devotee of gymnasiums, it has the active smell of all-day sweat, the perspiration of labor in a hot land. It takes me a second, but then I remember the Texas of my youth, on the Gulf Coast, and two-a-day football practices. The morning humidity baking the dew from the summer-green grass as the sun rose, the moisture rising but then becoming quickly trapped—at about chest-level—by the blanket of already-supersaturated air. Running, loose and limber, through that sky-soup of heat— perspiring, sure, gloriously so—and then taking a cool-down break, maybe not an actual nap but a ride in the car with the windows down, or riding our bicycles to a sandwich shop, or to get a milkshake, a hamburger, or cookies back at the house—we were always ravenous—and then before we knew it, it was time to be back on the field, running plays now, with the whistles and the slap of the ball and the creak and crack of plastic shoulderpads and the bighorn smack of cheap plastic helmets butting against one another; and sweat, once again, cascading down the small of the back in torrents.

Or if it was raining by then we would go into the weight room, which was no less humid, and sit or lie down on the various chairs and benches in order to contort ourselves into the requisite positions of rigor, straining and pushing and pulling, twisting and knotting, flexing and contracting with the day's second sweating. The sweat seeping from our salty skin again, not a sour smell and yet not entirely a fresh, new-made smell; a second-smell, but also a first. As long as we stayed active, it was not purely sour; it was the living scent of extreme exertions, punctuated by brief rests. It was the scent of an old world, the one that had first made us.

Beneath the green fronds, the scent is everywhere. It is like being in the same small room as the bearers of that scent, the ones undergoing the exertion.

And then suddenly there is a huge gorilla moving ahead of us, a silverback, the coal-black of his muscles the perfect complement to the green jungle, and it is precisely as if we have barged uninvited into his living room. He might have been expecting us, and he has no doubt had other such visitors before, but I get the sense that he's not exactly ready to give us a tour of the house yet. It's not so much that he's startled as it is that he wants a bit of distance until he gauges what we're about: until he gets a sense of how many of us there are, these pale strangers, with their strange scents, who have pretty much just come charging in through the undergrowth.

The first flash of thought in my mind—after the shock, of course—is that never have I seen anything like this in my life. Not grizzly bear, not elephant, not rhino or whale. Nothing.

The second flash is how huge and perfect his head is—how noble. The swaybacked muscle-clad body (and this is the third thought, how incredibly powerful he must be) is still gliding gracefully through the forest, rolling forward over small swales—but the head does not loll or sway, remains instead erect and fixed, secure. To be able to keep one's head so still while moving forward, over such uneven terrain, seems to me to create a conducive environment for the care and development of a significant, even massive amount of intelligence, and a great electrical complexity of emotions, a great electrical phalanx of spirit—and the guides gesture to us that it is okay to follow him, and now we see other gorillas moving through the forest all around us, also following the silverback, and we quicken our pace, not wanting them to leave.

How can the sight of something so unfamiliar—what we, with our limited worldview, cannot help but think of at first as surreal—be integrated into our new consciousness? We know the word *gorilla*, have grown up seeing fake representations of them in movies, and, on Halloween, seeing the occasional gorilla suit, shaggy and hot-seeming; but to be following them, choosing the same steps they are choosing and walking through the forest with them—and now they have settled down after our rude and unannounced intrusion, now they are sitting down and feeding, watching us with dignity and also some uncertainty and vexation; appalled, I think, at our manners, and seeming disapproving, disappointed, but tolerant—how do we put this new strangeness into our minds, where do we file it?

And all the more disorienting and wonderful is the fact that so much motion is involved: that we are not sitting in a blind, hidden from view, or in the back of a jeep, watching with binoculars, but instead—almost as if suddenly conscripted—are flowing with them through the forest, going wherever they go, and at their pace; stopping when they stop, and starting forward whenever they resume their trek. Walking together with them. How astonishingly kind of them to allow us to travel with them like this.

The sunlight is filtering down through the canopy, giving their jetblack coats a slightly iridescent quality. Never have I seen an animal so muscular; never have I seen a land animal more comfortable in its own body, more flexible and fluid. Why, evolutionarily, did we ever stand up? Look at us, next to them, teetering, with so many shifting and bulging disks, and our chattering, loose-sliding vertebrae, proceeding unsteadily forward!

As if one of the gorillas can divine my thoughts, he stands up and claps his palms to the iron plate of his chest, the great hands literally a blur, and at that close distance, the nothing-else-in-the-world-like-it sound rings gunshot-sharp upon us; and even as our senses are registering this, twining in our minds and being processed—the deep, sharp sound, the sight of the coal-black gorillas, the scent of the lush green forest that seems to so quickly absorb the chest-clapping—he has already dropped back down to all fours and is hurrying on. We stand there stunned to stillness. To have heard that magnificent and utterly unexpected drumbeat!

How can there only be 780 of them left in the world? How, in so vast and amazing a region, can we have saved for them only the cooling breath of these six extinct volcanoes, and this tiny park, this tiny garden, with these survivors moving through the volcano-made forest like the phantasmagoric last thoughts of the dying mountain, like the trailing-away vapors of the volcanoes' last breath?

I have not even yet said how big some of them are. They are all different sizes—they radiate the word *family*, with adolescents, mothers, scampering babies, all moving forward together—but the big ones are really big, certainly larger than any man—and again what is most arresting to me is their muscularity and grace. You may think you have seen these creatures before, but not like this. This is what has come through the eye of the needle; only something this perfect can pass through, and they move through their wet forest not with arrogance but humility, plucking the broad green leaves and peeling the wild celery and eating it with what seems like a considered meditation: as if, though they may not be continually amazed by the great bounty of their home and the security of their family around them, they do not take it for granted, either.

We have fifty-seven minutes left in paradise; fifty-six minutes, fifty-five. We gather in one spot along the new-made trail of their passage, some of us crouched and others of us leaning against vines and the boughs of trees we do not know the name of, and stare, not wanting to even blink, not believing what we are seeing. Some of them pass by so close that it seems we can feel their radiant body heat, the black fur holding the day's sun, five hundred pounds of life and intent.

It is an awful cliché to say that when we look at them, we are seeing at least some portion of ourselves reflected—that there are moments when it we might as well be looking in a mirror—but as with most clichés, there's an element of truth in that idea, if also an element of laziness and looseness. It is not quite like that. They are not ours, and we are not theirs. There is definitely a distance. But they are closer than anything you will have seen up to this point. They are the closest thing to us that we will ever know in this life. They are maybe not so much like brothers or sisters of ours as they are like close cousins, or like the children of brothers and sisters. I am not speaking now in metaphor, I realize; that is exactly what they are, but with the great authenticating scale of time attenuating that relationship in a way that paradoxically does not thin or dilute it. Certain ineradicable elements of our shared—what is the word? *Humanity? Spirit?*—have been preserved.

There is an understanding, but there is also a vast gulf. It is as if we left home such a long time ago, while they remained in the place where they were born. They have changed, too— they have accrued certain interior qualities, while abandoning or jettisoning others—but it cannot be said that in any way have they gotten lost, remaining here on this chain of old mountaintop volcanoes for so many millions of years. I think there are few who would disagree that we, for all of our rapid forward progress, have at times gotten lost ourselves. This may be one of the critical times in our evolutionary history where we feel more lost than we have ever been.

The gorillas are moving again. We surge, following the

black braid of them through the green. The guides watch the gorillas and us both, making sure we don't get too tangled in the braid: assessing the routes of each of us and each of them almost like little gods, trying to assess or prophesy future outcomes based on paths chosen. Fates, destinies.

And then the guides grow excited again; they are seeing something uncommon. The gorillas are circling around, they are making a wide loop, are leaving the park once more—they have decided to go back out into the fields, which is very unusual at any time, but particularly at this time of day.

They cross a deep ravine, then climb over the red lava-rock wall—one of them, an adolescent, walks along the wall for a while like a teenager balancing on railroad tracks, and another climbs to the top of a tree right at the edge of the park boundary and then leaps and swings back and forth, hanging always by only one arm, showing off. Were we ever even remotely that strong?

Frances tells us that some of them have been into the young green bamboo, and we see it now, out in the open plowed fields, a certain merriment to their demeanor, particularly in two of the babies—what we would call toddlers, if they were ours. The two little ones spin and wheel in crazy circles, then run up to their elders and whack them on the rump before scampering away, spinning around and around again, playing.

Are they going back out into the fields because they know that they can do so safely, accompanied now by our group of tourists? No one can say. Whatever the reason, they are having a gay old time. I imagine there might be almost no depression so profound that the sight of the babies' mad escapades, their rapturous embrace of the day, would not crack it open, filling the viewer with love and wonder and laughter. Some of the babies—newborns—ride on their mothers' backs like the tiniest of jockeys. Clutching so tightly, their blazing red eyes wide open, still so perpetually amazed by all that they see.

The big silverback—the Chief—stays up in the shade along the rock wall. Two of the bamboo-smitten youngsters start to follow him, as if momentarily considering giving him a butt-thwacking, but then wisely decide against it, and cartwheel down the hill instead, still electric with joy. The Chief sits down under a tree and gazes out at the fields, at the valley below and the mountains beyond, just sitting there, thinking.

The rest of us stand in the middle of the field, captivated and disbelieving, the soil loose beneath our feet. The villagers downslope pause again to watch us, and their body language seems to me to be not entirely approving; perhaps they are merely curious, but it seems to me to be a little more than that. Not fearful, but perhaps mildly resentful of our presence, though that feeling might be complicated, maybe, by the understanding that the gorillas, and our interest in them, are good for Rwanda.

How can there only be 780 of them left?

The junior silverback and a couple of adolescents, along with a mature female, have left the rock wall and are starting to tack downslope. Or that's what I think, anyway—Frances, however, perceives that they are actually angling our way, coming to check us out—bamboo-eaters!—and grows very alarmed, calling out to Lowry and me, who are kind of out on the wing of our formation, to come in closer, and to do so quickly.

Part of me is thinking, But you said not to make any quick movements around the gorillas, and part of me is thinking, Wow, it must be pretty urgent. And even as I am registering the alarm in his voice, still another part of me is thinking Look at how smart that was, they have the angle on us—with just a little bit of acceleration, they could cut us out from the herd.

Lowry's snapping pictures. Only now are the gorillas revealing what their plan had been all along—to come and play—and it is as Frances saw long before anyone else. I stop to let Lowry sweep in behind me, as if in a pick-and-roll, and just in the nick of time, our group's center is reconsolidated; the three truant gorillas, their bellies rumbling with fermented bamboo, veer away and continue on down the slope. As if that had been their intent all along.

They are all around us now, playing and wandering. Down below, a big mother continues to ride her infant around, like a human parent giving a horsey-ride. The Chief is still under his tree, observing his kingdom, and the juveniles are still walking along the wall, but now more and more of the band is heading straight down the slope, ever-farther into the new-earth of the plowed fields, spreading out and peeling the bark from what few spindly eucalyptus trees are still standing—trees that we now understand have been left here for a reason, or even replanted, following the clearing of the mountainside. With the dexterity of their fingers, and the power in their arms, they are not leaving anything untouched; they move from tree to tree deliberately, smacking their gums, licking the sap and chewing and peeling. Party time. A pregnant female climbs a bow-shaped eucalyptus and appears to use its weight to stretch her back, which must be aching from the front-load of her ponderous breasts and hugely expectant belly.

Perhaps the farmers, who stand below, leaning on their hoes and watching stoically, see it as ruin; we Westerners have the luxury of seeing it as something else. Again, while it did not occur to me in the moment, I can't help but wonder now if it was our presence that gave these creatures the cover they needed, the boldness to go down into the fields and lay waste—though *waste* is not quite the precise word—to all those eucalyptus. It seems not to be a sustainable venture—if the gorillas did that every day, there's no telling how far their momentum would carry them. But then the eucalyptus were never native in the first place; perhaps the gorillas see them as sweet weeds.

How big does a park need to be to hold and nurture gorillas? How large does the earth need to be to hold and nurture us?

One of the mothers has, for whatever reason, left off from the eucalyptus frenzy and come back over to where we're still standing. We're surrounded by gorillas, we're in a sea of gorillas—they are going about their daily lives, roughly circling us like slow electrons—and she settles into the grass beside the rock wall of the park boundary, not fifteen yards away from us. The tiny baby that has been riding on her back dismounts and climbs up into her arms, and she sits there watching us with what can only be described as a kind and wise and loving expression, grooming her baby's fuzzy little head, noting with pride, it seems, everything that is perfect about him—his tiny, perfectly formed ears, more humanlike than our own, and his tiny fingers, likewise. His bright red inquisitive eyes, his cute little nose. She is in bliss, she is in love, and she wants us to admire him, and wants something else from us too, I think, though even now I cannot quite say what it was. I have not given up on thinking about it, and wondering, and trying to figure it out.

We didn't pursue her. She came back up here to us.

With the practiced movement so familiar to our own species, she half-scoops the baby up to her breast even as he is climbing up into her lap, ascending; she offers him a Madonna look as he curls in against her, looking down at him blissfully, smiling, plucking idly at the hair on his head, trying to get him just perfect. But he *is* perfect; there is nothing more that can be improved. From time to time she beholds us, fixes us with her steady, loving gaze, and in the presence of that gaze, and her quiet rapture, I feel that we might somehow be capable of coming slowly to understand all that we might care to know about ourselves, and that the only restraint upon that knowledge might indeed be our own failure of nerve: an unwillingness to fully embrace or accept all that is within us, and that she can so plainly see.

She is not in love with us. She is in love with her infant. But when she looks at us, she is seeing us in a way—seeing us with a deeper knowledge than we are used to. It is all the more remarkable—breathtaking, really—for its lack of judgment.

Sixteen minutes in paradise; fifteen minutes, fourteen.

I don't know how long we watch her. It feels like a long time. It doesn't feel like we are being voyeurs, because again it is she who has ferried her baby up the hill to us; I don't know what it feels like. It is amazing, it is hypnotic, and yet—for me, the eternal worrier—there is just the faintest touch of discomfort. Part of me worries that she is mistaken—that she is seeing more in us than there really is. There's no way we are capable of being that deserving; perhaps she is seeing too little, seeing only the good, only the best.

But she has been here too long for that, as has her kind. She sees our wonder, our amazement, our joy and our confusion—

sees our delighted puzzlement—and she beholds it all with compassion.

It is Frances who calls us away. More and more of the other gorillas are drifting downslope, feeding on the eucalyptus bark, and reluctantly, but also not wanting to overstay our welcome—wanting to give her the sweet indulgence of time uninterrupted by visitors, admirers—we follow Frances down through the fields of loose soil, down to where the others are peeling bark and climbing the slender young trees.

One adolescent is climbing up a pole-sized trunk, tugging on the long strands of fraying bark, but he hasn't yet mastered the technique—he ends up just kind of hanging there, as if dangling from a rope swing. The number-two silverback—an incredibly muscled individual, beautifully bound up with improbable curves of brawn that are no less supple for their thickness—approaches him oh-so-casually. With the glee of youth, he pretends to ascend the little tree nonchalantly, to show the adolescent how it's done—anyone can see how eager the silverback is to demonstrate his power, his great confidence in the world—his mastery—and thus it is that with *brio*, and perhaps still not yet fully understanding his own strength, despite his pride and pleasure in his awareness of it, he climbs a little too high on the inward side of the trunk and pulls back on it a little too hard; the tree bends and bows like a fishing pole, surely it's going to snap—nothing can be that limber—and yet still the silverback continues to ride it out, swaying way back, way back—the tree is a perfect upside-down letter C, with the giant gorilla inverted within the belly of it, feet and hands gripping the tree and straining against it—and of course it's at that point that the tree breaks in half, which sends him plummeting, a gorilla cannonball, still clutching the top half of the eucalyptus.

He lands heavily in the soft soil, and—you have to hand it to him—looks up quickly at his protégé, and then decides to go with it; leaning back as if in a lounge chair and lifting the entire upper half of the tree—about the length of a pole-vaulter's pole—to his lips. And then, with biceps bulging and gleaming in the sun, he begins to chew.

All around us—wherever there is a small and isolated eucalyptus—the trees are shaking, the gorillas gripping them like giant lollipops. They move through the low troughs and crests of newly turned earth looking every bit like laborers in those fields themselves; the muscles in their backs rise and fall, rolling up, it seems, in the exact shape of the earth below them, so that it is possible to believe they are being born right before us, rising up out of the black ground, a crop being raised, and set in motion. And it looks, too, as they move across the fields on all fours, as if they are kneading and shaping the soil into the shape of themselves, of the world—making the whole world itself, with them in it. An empty garden, with only them in it. Or only them and us, and all the rest of the garden waiting to be filled.

What if we are not the light? What if we are the darkness, the serpent who came in so late? What if we long to be good—*aspire* to be good—but good is not our true nature?

Five minutes in paradise; four minutes, three.

Frances informs us crisply, formally, of our imminent time limit, and then, as if in a dream, at the one-minute mark, the gorillas below us rise from their languor, and, like factory workers summoned in from break by a whistle only they can hear, begin moving away, toward the park. Twenty or more gorilla backs, all converging into one larger group, walking together, humble once more, heading back into the forest, and leaving us behind, still out in the fields, exposed, vulnerable, transformed. Our time is up.

We don't talk much, on the way down; we walk in single-file, past all the farmers. Something feels terrible, and something feels wonderful. It's very confusing. Is it like a dream, or is everything else like a dream, and this one hour, an awakening?

We would have liked to have stayed longer. Walking out, and then driving out, we feel acutely the distance between us and them widening, our time with them receding; and although there is a bit of the old human loneliness that is so much a part and parcel of leavetaking, there is something different accompanying it this time, something positive and powerful. It is a feeling of having been gilded: having been brushed and coated with something strong and special, something which, if we will only hold it within us, can help us in our lives from now on.

Fretter that I am, I worry that that residue—which we have all felt, if but occasionally, before—will dissipate, evaporate, and I try hard to lock it in, to hoard it, to hold it. So strong is the feeling of awe, of reverence and wonder—particularly when recalling the look of the Madonna mother as she nursed her baby—that it seems that this soul-filled feeling can never go away; and yet I know from past experience that it does. Always, it does, and then you have to go and get it back.

*   *   *

Sometimes Frances is called upon to go in with the biologists to capture a gorilla in order to draw a blood sample, for research. It's very dangerous work, he says, going in with the pistol with its tranquilizer dart, "because if the chief sees it, he fights." The biologists have to scare the other gorillas away, and isolate the one they want to sample, and then dart it quickly, and draw the blood quickly, before the rest of the gorillas see the operation. The gorillas don't understand that the biologists might want to help them. When they see the gun, they get very angry and afraid. They'll fight to the death to defend their own, and they cannot conceive that a human being with a gun is in any way a good thing.

We arrive back at the lodge in time for a late lunch—a delicious tomato bisque, a fresh salad, olives. We wander the flower gardens, entranced, watch the jeweled birds, the honey creepers, flitting and darting. We sit on our porch and visit, murmuring quietly; we lie on the lawn and read; we nap. Time does not seem to exist. In the garden, I find a giant *Cecropia* moth, day-stunned and disoriented, his lovely black-and-russet owl-eyed wings still spread open. At first I think he's dead—he's brown and furry, like a mammal—a small bat—and I pick him up to show the others, but when I do so, he stirs as if resurrected, returning to life as in a fable. What a fable that would be, if we carried within us the ability to summon and even resurrect life, rather than simply to take it away.

Still holding on to my discovery, I bring him over to

my companions—showing them the feathery, ultrasensitive antennae, the inquisitive night eyes, and the round head, so much like that of a more conscious creature—and then carry him farther down into the garden, to a place of cool shade, where he might rest and gather his strength before evening.

As if no less fragile than my moth, we spend the next few hours resting and recovering from all that we have seen thus far, the sublime and the macabre. We have traveled beyond our borders, and all we want to do now is sit quietly, and watch the splendid towering cumulus clouds swelling ever upward, and think. How fortunate that we have found a place where we can do so. Now and again a gardener walks past, watering one plant or another, making certain tiny adjustments to paradise, but for the most part the garden is entirely ours for the day.

We nap, we dine again. We walk from our cottages across the narrow suspension bridge to the elegant woven-grass dining area and then back again, with the sky clear and fresh-smelling following a brief but spectacular thunderstorm. The stars are fierce. We sleep soundly, as if buoyed on a bed of peace.

In the morning we are awakened by a sound like waves, though we are so far from any ocean; no ocean touches this country's borders.

We walk out onto the porch and see that far in the distance there is a school, and that the sound we're hearing is hundreds of children laughing and running out onto a vast soccer field lit with a coppery gold light, still dew-clad. The children are not playing soccer; they are simply chasing one another, running back and forth, playing and clapping their hands and singing.

It's a pretty wonderful sound to wake up to, and an equally lovely sight. We stand there in that perfect garden, in that early gold light, the rising sun in our eyes burning the dew off the ground so that steam rises in burning shrouds all around us, and look down at the waves of distant laughing children—at them wheeling back and forth like shorebirds along the strand line, shrieking. If you were watching from some farther vantage, it would be possible to believe that they were fleeing something, screaming and running in scattered, terrified chaos, but they are only playing this morning; each of them as filled with joy, it seems, as the human body is capable of being. We stand there for a long time, mesmerized by the great beauty, and are completely unwilling to leave. We know we can't go down there and join them, but it's almost enough to stand there in the garden and just watch.

WRITING FROM THE
BUTARE WORKSHOP

WHAT DOES THIS MEAN?

by BONAVENTURE IYAMUDUHAYE

Since the day of my birth, I've never seen this
When I was still young, I thought this cannot be
I don't believe it, I'm not part of it
I asked them, young and old people
But no one could tell me. What does this mean?

Where have you seen a lion, fighting a little fly?
Where have you seen a hunter, killing an ant?
How is a bull eager
To have sex with a calf? I burst into tears,
I cry for them. What does this mean?

I blame my God, who closes his eyes
While this is happening. I blame myself
For my being on earth, weakened by the devil;
I'm afraid of the jungle, full of wild animals
No one comes to rescue them. What does this mean?

How many kilometers is a girl obliged to walk
Before she is called a boy? How long
Do I have to say this, to have those flies released
From the lion's teeth? Don't think I'm crazy
I'm compelled to ask. What does this mean?

I sympathize for them, I speak for them
Those beloved innocent, who could be treated well
They are fed up with cocks, which violate them
They are still too young, they want to grow up
I don't understand. What does this mean?

What makes me cry is not a little thing
It is very shameful, to eat an uncooked meal
When the cooked one is ready. How can I keep
Quiet and cross my arms, while the future of the
World is still at risk? What does this mean?

I AM KILLED ALIVE

by AMINI NGABONZIZA

I am seeing death wherever I am. I am listening to death whenever I dream. I am touching death in whatever I handle. They say I am traumatized, but I am killed alive.

The killers caused my fall. They came to my home with death in hand. Armed with machetes, I was killed alive.

With machetes they picked my father like a tithe. I was filled with sorrow and cried to him, "Father! They'll kill you, Father!" One killer took my arm, and kicked me once.

My father tried to save me, but he met his end. The killer stood above him. One machete strike to his neck. I am killed alive.

They say it happened long ago. But I see it now, in these days. I saw the second militia not far, approaching my weeping mother, pregnant then.

One killer asked another, "How can we kill this pregnant mother?" The other said, "We must! We must kill all Tutsis with their roots."

He said, "We will be like medical doctors. With our sword we will carve out the one to kill, then the mother." What an atrocity! The surgery! I am killed alive!

I watched the death of my family, bombed and macheted, small parts of kids, lamenting without a savior. Raped sisters, tired grandmothers weeping for help. Silent survivors.

What kind of death? What kind of crime? To be killed just because I am Tutsi! From the womb of my mother I chose nothing. I was born Tutsi and couldn't change my violent fate.

I am killed alive. My wounds are fresh. What can I do? What can I think when I see the ones who killed my mother and father go unpunished?

To be angry is not enough. To feel lonely is to crumble. I am killed breathing. No one to bury me. No one to witness. I am killed alive.

MY HOME

by ANNE-MARIE NYIRANSANGA

My home is not
Like this world
Where I cry and cry
So much of the time
Where I miss peace
Where I miss joy
Where I miss happiness.
My home is placed
Somewhere beyond the blue.
In my home
There is no more sorrow
In my home
There is no more pain
In my home
There are no lost
beloved ones

In my home
There is no more sadness.
In my home
I will not be
Unhappy again.
Oh! When shall I see
My home?

THE LONG NIGHTS

by DIEUDONNÉ NIYONIZERA

I

IT WAS EVENING, the sun about to set. Karemangingo was sitting on a stool near the door. The children had come home from school. The evening activities for the elder siblings had started, and the little children were playing their last game of the day.

Karemangingo called to his elder daughter Umwiza, who was crushing some cassava in a mortar to make *ugali* for their dinner. Karemangingo wanted to listen to the radio, to know the current news.

"Yesterday I heard that the president of the republic has gone to Arusha, to negotiate with the RPF," Karemangingo said. "But I do not know if he has come back. So I have to pass the night knowing what goes on around the country."

No sooner had he turned on RTLM, though, than he heard bad news.

"Yesterday evening the airplane that transported the president of the republic crashed at the airport," the journalist was saying. "There is do doubt that it was the RPF that shot it. Now decisions have been made: all the Tutsis are to be killed. Hunt them to their last number! There is no distinction. From the oldest to the newborn child. All have to be killed!

"But who will do the work? You Hutus are required to get involved. Especially *interahamwe*: remember the training you have been given. You let the Tutsis live, and you will die as your president did!"

As Karemangingo was still listening, not knowing what was next, he heard shouts from outside the fence. It was a crowd of killers, *interahamwe*.

"We are killing snakes today!" shouted Bamara, the group commander.

"What?" Karemangingo said.

"Tutsis are snakes, and before the night passes away, we will have killed them all!" Bamara replied. "Cleared their names from our land! The sentence is given. The government has ordered it. Today you will know that it is not for nothing that we *interahamwe* have been trained!"

Bamara had not yet finished his speech when his followers started pulling the house down and beating the children to death. Rukara struck Karemangingo with a machete. He cut into his head, and the man died on the spot.

It was hard to escape. Only God could save souls. Umiza was raped and badly wounded, but was able to flee; of the other children, only Kayitesi and Kibaruta managed to escape before the violence, while Nziza and Nsenga were killed. But even in death, each soul has its story.

*   *   *

Kayitesi and Kibaruta were lying in the banana yard. The sky had turned gloomy, and their hearts beat at a frantic pace. The anti-erosion channels had become their home. Banana leaves had become their cover. At 9 p.m., it started to rain stones.

The thunder groaned, and the lightning became violent. The poor children could hear nothing but groaning, and the crushed banana-tree leaves falling. The wind picked up, and soon the channels were filled with water.

The children could do nothing. Their home had been destroyed and turned to ruins.

At midnight, the rain stopped, but their confusion only increased. The little boy, Kibaruta, suggested going back home: that was his childish suggestion. He thought they could light the fire for warmth or even cook the dinner that they had left uncooked. His elder sister denied the suggestion.

Though they had become wet and the cold was increasing, she hoped the sky would remain dark. The killers had departed, but the banana yard could not continue to be a refuge for the children. The morning would come soon, and the killers would start their hunting anew.

Desolated, the children stood up. No human voice could be heard—only the sounds of wild animals, of reptiles and insects. Kayitesi took the hand of the little boy, and then they started running.

The night was as dark as charcoal and the path itself like a cave. The more they ran, the more they fell down; the earth had turned into mud.

"Oh my God! I don't think we'll survive!" Kayitesi said.

"We will be eaten by animals, or killed by enemies, or we will die of hunger!"

Her mind was full of acrobatics. And then a new idea appeared.

"We have our maternal aunt who lives in Karasa village," she said. "We shall go there. Maybe we shall find a refuge."

As soon as the idea came into her mind, Kayitesi told the young boy Kibaruta that they were turning around and starting out toward their aunt's. Karasa was about fifteen kilometers from Kagezi, the village of Kayitesi and Kibaruta. They would have to move quickly to reach it before sunrise.

Hearts beating, their cold and hunger mixed with fear, they followed the road to Karasa. On their way, they heard some strides from within the bush; they could not see the person. Their fear rose up, and they started running again to save their lives. The moon had begun to give its light, since the clouds were no longer in the sky.

The two children had hardly started to run when they heard a voice calling their names. It was their sister, Umwiza, who had escaped despite her wounds. When they realized it was her, they turned back.

She could hardly speak, but she told them both the course of the incident: how their father and two brothers had been killed, how she had been raped and wounded, how the house had been plundered and destroyed, the domestic animals slaughtered, and so forth.

Kayitesi decided that she would help Umwiza to walk. But the more they advanced, the harder it became. After they had marched some five hundred meters, Umwiza started crying.

"Oh, my sister, I am dying!" she said. "If only I could have some water to drink."

"We cannot get any water in this area," Kayitesi replied. "Be strong. Maybe at Aunt Maria's we'll get some."

With much difficulty, they continued on their way. But after a walk of about ten minutes, Umwiza cried her last cry, asking for water. Her soul departed. Umwiza was dead.

Kayitesi said, "Oh my God! This is what it means to be called Tutsi. I wonder who coined such a name! Why are we dying like this?"

"Umwiza! Stand up," the little boy called. He did not know that his sister had died.

Kayitesi's anxiety increased as the little boy continued to shout. It was like a sharpened sword in her heart. And almost immediately, a new dilemma arose: should they leave their dead sister on the path? Should they stay at her side? They would be waiting for nothing but death. Could they ask for help from the nearby homes? Many of them might be involved in the killings. There was no choice but to leave the corpse behind, and continue on their way.

Kayitesi took the little boy's hand again and forced him to walk. As they marched on, the boy asked his sister, "Why did we leave Umwiza sleeping there?"

"She is dead," Kayitesi answered.

"Why is she dead?"

"She is dead because the *interahamwe* wounded her."

"But why are they killing us? Didn't I see that all who came to kill us were our neighbors? Did we insult or harm any of them?"

"No."

"Why then are they killing us?"

"They are killing us simply because they say we are Tutsis. They say we are conspiring with the RPF, who invaded Rwanda."

"Why did they invade?"

"Because they were denied the right to come back and live in Rwanda after they were forced to flee from this country many years ago by the newly formed government, which said that they were taking revenge on the Tutsis who had dominated the Hutus for so long."

"But could that be a sound reason for killings?"

"Even I myself cannot understand," Kayitesi said. "We are victims of bad leadership and political domination."

"Who do you think has made the engine start?" the boy asked.

"Many people are involved. First, there are the colonialists who established the divide-and-rule policy. They planted segregation in the country. Then there are the bad leaders who thought they were leaders of just one part, not of all Rwandan people. They became tyrannical, because they thought others were their enemies."

"I think I understand," the boy said, "but not all. The other questions, I'll ask our aunt once we've arrived. Maybe in her house we shall survive."

"The problems are still complicated," Kayitesi said. "Our aunt is also called Tutsi. She is also on the run. But her husband is called Hutu, and he is a good man. He cannot invest in evil actions. I hope we shall survive there."

It was about 3 a.m. when they arrived at Karasa village. Kayitesi knocked at the door and Aunt Maria opened it. Maria was strongly touched when she saw how the children had become dirty and were trembling from the cold and fear. She changed their clothes, washed their feet, and covered them with a blanket. Then she went to the kitchen to make some ugali and soup for them.

After a while, all was ready, and Aunt Maria started asking them about the rest of their family. Kayitesi told her what had happened, and their aunt was filled with grief. The acrobatics started in her mind. For a few minutes, she was talking to herself.

My husband is a good man. I know he is.

He is a confirmed Christian with moral qualities.

He cannot invest in betrayal, nor in killings.

I know he loves me. So he loves my relatives as well.

But the problem is hard.

Hiding a person is not easy. Our house is always suspected.

Even I myself am a candidate for killing.

Still confused, a new idea came into Aunt Maria's mind. She had seen other Tutsis heading for the district headquarters last evening, because the story had gone around that the district had agreed to provide refuge for them. She did not know it was a trick.

Maria suggested that she accompany the two children to the district headquarters, and promised to visit them there whenever possible. Kayitesi accepted the idea, and Maria, together with her husband Neza, took them there before the morning came. They gave them some food, a blanket, a jerry-can, and a pan to be used for cooking.

At the district headquarters, the children were received by a policeman who showed them the house where others were being kept. Inside everyone was desolate, and could hardly speak. Men, women, children, and the elderly were all being kept together. It was a concentration camp.

One old man called Sheja saw the children and welcomed them. "Tell us about the outside," he said. After Kayitesi explained their story, Sheja realized that he knew Kare-mangingo, the children's father. He decided to keep them by his side for as long as they stayed in the district headquarters.

The life there was harsh. Neither water nor food was offered to the refugees. Children began to starve, and old people grew weaker and weaker. Fifteen days after the camp was opened, the district authorities decided to kill all the refugees.

It was evening, about 5 p.m. Groups of *interahamwe* and policemen were brought to the camp with their weapons and whistles. Traditional arms were supported by modern ones. At five sharp, Rumanura, the head of the *interahamwe*, gave the order, and his men opened fire.

The poor Tutsis were exterminated. Could anyone survive? Only God can tell. After firing their weapons, the killers entered with machetes, spears, and clubs, without forgetting bows and arrows. They killed the rest of the refugees, the ones who had survived.

By nightfall, they thought that all had been killed, and left, everyone returning to their home with their loads of plunder.

Kayitesi and Kibaruta had managed to survive. They were lying on the ground among the dead bodies, wounded. Kayitesi was wounded in her ribs, and Kibaruta was wounded on his head, between his right ear and eye. It was about midnight when Kayitesi noticed that she was breathing. She stretched her hand out and noticed that the little boy was breathing, too.

The next day Aunt Maria and her husband heard that a few people might have survived the killings in the district headquarters. They decided to look for the children.

By chance, they found them in the house of a generous Hutu man who had received and hidden them. He lived near the district headquarters, and his name was Mahoro. When Maria and her husband arrived, he agreed to return the two children to them.

The situation was difficult. The wounds in Kayitesi's ribs were like holes. When she was given a cup of tea, it could pass through the wounds and come out.

"I'm… I don't know if they will survive," Aunt Maria said to her husband.

"We will try our best to treat them," her husband said. "No one knows—maybe God will help and make them survive. The fact that they escaped is the first sign."

With many difficulties, Aunt Maria and Neza managed to reach home with the wounded survivors at midnight. Maria started heating some water to wash the children's bodies, and prepared some porridge for them. She attempted to treat their wounds, though she had no medical supplies. Maria lived by hiding; at any time, she knew, things could change again.

As the time went by, the situation did begin to change. All the Tutsi houses had been destroyed, and no one thought that any Tutsi could have escaped without being killed. But in the bush, some had survived, and were still running. Two months later, the story went around that the RPF was advancing to stop the genocide.

The district headquarters in each area were the first to be

conquered. The *interahamwe* and the army were defeated and fled. Whenever they conquered an area, the RPF called on the people to come and live in camps to be assured security. When Aunt Maria heard this, she told her husband, and they went to stay in the Karasa camp together with their four children and the two orphans.

Genocide was put to an end in the area, and later on in the whole country. A new government was formed, and given the name Government of National Unity. The process of rebuilding the country started then, and later the repatriation of refugees was put into action.

Though her wounds were healed on the outside, they remained fresh in Kayitesi's body. Particles of grenades tormented her from time to time. Vulnerable, the two children remained. Without a place to call home. Like eggs without shells, they felt.

At school it was hard for the little boy to grasp anything. Kayitesi could never drink water, because whenever she took up a cup of water, she remembered her sister Umwiza, who in her last breath had cried out: "Give me some water to drink!" It was as if Kayitesi had gotten the water for her sister, only to find that she was not there.

The body damaged, the psyche damaged.

ACKNOWLEDGMENTS

This trip remains in some ways the proverbial blur of images and emotions, and in other ways a series of indelible moments. For my gratitude toward the many people who helped with the project, I find I can construct no ordered structure or narrative. Every time I needed something or asked for it, I received it. Terry Tempest Williams first suggested that I might find something if I went to Rwanda, and that she wanted my daughter Lowry to see that something as well—and she was, in her lovely way of intuition and observation, correct about this. I and my family thank Terry for accompanying us, and for leading us.

Numerous supporters in Missoula helped make the trip possible—Dr. Georgia Milan of St. Patrick's Hospital, Deb Hicks, Allison Troxel, Cary Griffin, and Yvonne and Jeffrey Gritzner. I couldn't have made it without their belief that this was a trip worth taking. Missoula Community Access Television provided the use of a camera, which is appreciated.

I'm grateful to the editors at *McSweeney's*—particularly Jordan Bass—and at *Orion*—Jennifer Sahn—who supported the trip with assignments that helped defray the cost. I also am grateful to my editor at Houghton Mifflin Harcourt, Nicole Angeloro, for providing me with a hundred copies of one of my earlier books to donate to students in the writing club in Butare, and to Tato Sumantri of Wipf and Stock Publishers and Russell Perreault at Vintage for providing copies of Terry's books, as well. And I am indebted to other authors who have visited—or lived in—and written about Rwanda, including George Schaller, Immaculée Ilibagiza, and Philip Gourevitch. Terry also pitched in to fill in what my memory erased.

Anders Brooker, manager and owner of the Runner's Edge, was incredibly generous with his gift of dozens of fine running shoes for children in the Twa village outside of Gisenyi, as was Nike, through the assistance of Dennis Haddad and Scott Slovic. Nora Gallagher helped coordinate Patagonia's assistance with luggage for transport of books and shoes; Carolyn Rothberg of Plaza Travel was indispensable and caring, and is surely the best in her business.

In Rwanda, where to begin? Louis Gakumba and his family—Erast Karere, Gasimbi Innocent, and Alexander Kamusore among them—helped us achieve ambitious logistical goals and provided meaningful background, context, history, and perception. And Louis, together with the passionate and dynamic Amini Ngabonziza, president of the National University of Rwanda's Linguistics and Literature Student Association, performed great work in assembling the Butare writing club; it was an honor to speak and be with those extraordinary brave and talented students, and we remain moved by the dedication of their mentor, Professor François Ntaganda. Elizabeth Mujawamariya, our empathetic and intelligent guide at Nyamata, Eric Reynolds, and his fiancée, Mariam Uwizeyimana, were wonderful company and hosts, as was Rukirande Musana Jean Bosco of the Red Cross. The assistance of artist Lily Yeh and photographer Teresa Yeh in delivering shoes to the Twa village was invaluable. In Virunga

National Park, our guide Frances Ndagijimana of Goldenland Safaris is a gifted professional—it was our great luck to be helped by him, and by our tracker, Jerome Ndabereye.

I know that to a reader all of these may be just names, formalities in the code of gratitude. But writing them, I am humbled by the graciousness and integrity of all I encountered. No one who visits Rwanda can avoid being changed forever; that we are all too late in our arrival is all the more poignant. There can be sorrow in knowledge, but it is undeniable that there can also be great beauty. Nowhere else have I seen the two so twined.

RICK BASS is the author of twenty-nine other books, including *The Black Rhinos of Namibia* and *A Thousand Deer*, both of which will be published later this year. He has received fellowships from the National Endowment for the Arts and the Guggenheim Foundation; his stories have received O. Henry Awards and numerous Pushcart Prizes. Most recently, his memoir *Why I Came West* was a finalist for a National Book Critics Circle Award. He lives in Montana.